FILLED

DAVE WILLIAMS

FILLED:

*How You Can Be Filled
With The Mightiest Power
In The Universe*

DAVE WILLIAMS

Filled
How You Can Be Filled With The Mightiest Power In The Universe

Unless otherwise indicated, all scripture quotations are taken from the King James Version of the Bible.

First Printing 2002

Published by

DECAPOLIS PUBLISHING

Printed in the United States of America

BOOKS BY DAVE WILLIAMS

ABCs Of Success And Happiness
AIDS Plague
Art of Pacesetting Leadership
Beauty Of Holiness
Christian Job Hunter's Handbook
Desires Of Your Heart
Depression, Cave Of Torment
Genuine Prosperity, The Power To Get Wealth
Getting To Know Your Heavenly Father
Gifts That Shape Your Life And Change Your World
Grand Finale Revival
Grief And Mourning
Growing Up In Our Father's Family
Have You Heard From the Lord Lately?
How To Be A High Performance Believer
Laying On Of Hands
Lonely In The Midst Of A Crowd
Miracle Results Of Fasting
The New Life . . . The Start Of Something Wonderful
La Nueva Vida (The New Life . . . SPANISH)
The Pastor's Pay
Patient Determination
The Road To Radical Riches
Revival Power Of Music
Secret Of Power With God
Seven Signposts On The Road To Spiritual Maturity
Slain In The Spirit — Real Or Fake?
Somebody Out There Needs You
Success Principles From The Lips Of Jesus
Supernatural Soulwinning
Thirty-Six Minutes With The Pastor
Tongues And Interpretation
Understanding Spiritual Gifts
What To Do If You Miss The Rapture
World Beyond- The Mysteries of Heaven
Your Pastor - Key To Your Personal Wealth

Contents

Introduction: The Mightiest Power In The Universe 11

1. *Holy Spirit Night* 21

2. *The Whole Ball Of Wax?* 27

3. *Doctrine Of Baptisms* 33

4. *The Lightning Of God* 41

5. *Who Can We Believe?* 59

6. *What Must I Do To Receive?* 69

7. *Overflowing Power And Joy* 87

8. *Ten Big Benefits* 99

9. *Tongues: The Big Controversy* 121

10. *Two Big Myths Exposed* 137

11. *Passive Belief Or Active Faith?* 149

12. *Stepping Into The Third Dimension* 161

13. *Instructions For Being Filled* 171

14. *Your Unlimited Potential In The Holy Spirit* 183

Endnotes 196

About The Author 198

"You may as well try to see without eyes, hear without ears, or breathe without lungs as to try to live the Christian life without being filled with the Spirit."

— D.L. Moody

Introduction

THE MIGHTIEST POWER IN THE UNIVERSE

Have you ever wondered why you rarely see any of the kinds of miracles you read about in the Bible?

Do you have a heart for God but somehow feel unfulfilled in your relationship with Him?

Do you believe it's possible to duplicate the miracles of Jesus in our modern times? Or do you believe that miracles, signs, wonders, and gifts of the Holy Spirit all passed away with the first apostles?

IS SOMETHING MISSING?

If believers today are truly baptized with the Holy Spirit, then *where is the power Jesus promised?* Could it be that we are missing something? Is it possible that Christians today are stopping short of some deeper dimension in spiritual things? I believe this is precisely the case.

> And, being assembled together with *them*, commanded them that they should not depart from Jerusalem, but wait for the promise of the Father, which, *saith he*, ye have heard of me. For John truly baptized with water; but ye shall be baptized with the Holy Ghost not many days hence. BUT YE SHALL RECEIVE POWER, after that the Holy Ghost is come upon you: and ye shall be witnesses unto me both in Jerusalem, and in all Judaea, and in Samaria, and unto the uttermost part of the earth.
>
> — Acts 1:4-5,8

> Verily, verily, I say unto you, He that believeth on me, the works that I do shall he do also; and GREATER *WORKS* THAN THESE SHALL HE DO; because I go unto my Father.
>
> — John 14:12

All true believers have already experienced the baptism *of* the Holy Spirit.[1] That is the second dimensional relationship with the Holy Spirit when He comes to abide *in* you at the time of salvation.[2]

I know at this point many of my evangelical friends are saying, "Pastor Williams has seen the light." While at the same time my Pentecostal friends are calling me a "heretic." But wait a minute. Give me a chance to explain what I mean.

The Bible teaches us about *three* different relationships with the Holy Spirit, which we will discuss in a moment.

First, however, we must remember that it is the Holy Spirit who brings us the *power* to be effective witnesses of Christ. It was the Holy Spirit's *power* working through the first century believers that brought miracles, healings, and massive evangelism, accompanied by signs and wonders.

Not only did the apostles, through this enduement[3] of *power*, bring astonishing miracles to many hurting lives, but Spirit-filled laymen like Phillip and Stephen also performed signs and wonders as a witness to Jesus Christ's love and mercy. Masses of people witnessed the Risen Jesus as they beheld miracles being wrought by first century Christians. This must have been that *power* Jesus promised to His followers just before He ascended to heaven.[4]

But where is that power today? If we believe that Jesus Christ is the same yesterday, today, and forever (Hebrews 13:8), then where is that promised power for His followers now?

THE THREE DIMENSIONS OF RELATIONSHIP

I believe that power is found in the third dimensional relationship with the Holy Spirit. Every believer has experienced the second dimensional relationship with the Holy Spirit, but not all have received the third dimensional relationship.

Let me explain:

■ *1. The first dimensional relationship with the Holy Spirit* is the only association a sinner (or unbeliever) has with the Holy Spirit. This relationship is that of the condemned sinner with the One who convinces and convicts the sinner of his sins (John 16:8-11).

When Peter preached his first sermon after being filled with the Holy Spirit, who was it that "pricked" his listener's hearts? It was the Holy Spirit. He was *with* the listeners but not *in* them.

The Holy Spirit didn't come to condemn the sinner but to convince the sinner of his need for the Savior.[5] The Holy Spirit is *with* the unbeliever, working on his heart as he hears the message of the Gospel.

What a wonderful blessing to know the Holy Spirit is *with* our unsaved family members and friends, working to convince them of their need for Jesus Christ.

In one sense, He is like a compassionate prosecutor. He points out your sins, declaring you guilty and fit for hell, yet offers you a wonderful way of being declared, "not guilty." The Holy Spirit proclaims, "Yes, every person on earth is guilty and worthy of hell, but the gift of God is eternal life through

Jesus Christ."[6] He gently pricks the hearts of sinners and works to draw them to Jesus. This is the first relationship a person will have with the Holy Spirit.

■ *2. The second dimensional relationship with the Holy Spirit* is when a sinner turns from his sins and receives Jesus Christ. The Holy Spirit is *with* the unbeliever but, at the point of turning to Christ, the Holy Spirit comes *into* the new believer's heart and life.

When Peter's listeners, in Acts chapter two, heard the Gospel preached it was then that the Holy Spirit "pricked" their hearts (Acts 2:37). Three thousand men paid attention to that "pricking" and received Christ that day and immediately they were supernaturally baptized *by* the Holy Spirit into the body of Christ; the Church (1 Corinthians 12:13). This was the baptism *of* the Holy Spirit, or, the *second dimensional relationship* with the Holy Spirit.

Every person who has a second dimensional relationship with the Holy Spirit is sealed and marked for eternity (Ephesians 1:13). Heaven will one day be his home. This is a wonderful condition and, from a personal standpoint, the most important by far. But sadly, many of God's precious children have been operating on *limited power* because they haven't yet stepped into the third dimension. This power is available to all true followers of Christ.

■ *3. The third dimensional relationship with the Holy Spirit* is when we are baptized *with* the Holy Spirit. The baptism *with* the Holy Spirit is very different than the baptism *of* the Holy Spirit. The baptism *of* the Holy Spirit is when the Holy Spirit baptizes you into the body of Christ.[7] The baptism *with* the Holy Spirit is when Jesus Himself fills you to overflowing with a *power* from Heaven to accomplish God's miracle purposes in people's lives here on the earth.[8]

There are different scriptural phrases that speak of this third dimensional life:

1. The baptism in the Holy Spirit (Matthew 3:11).

2. The baptism with the Holy Spirit (Luke 3:16; Acts 1:4, 5, 8).

3. The enduement of power from on high (Luke 24:49).

4. The infilling of the Holy Spirit (Acts 2:4; Ephesians 5:18).

5. Rivers of living water (John 7:38, 39).

6. The gift of the Holy Ghost (Acts 2:38, 39; Acts 10:44-46).

7. The Promise of the Father (Luke 24:49).

8. The Holy Ghost coming upon you (Acts 19:6).

THE MIGHTIEST POWER IN THE UNIVERSE

Peloubet, in his commentary on Matthew, calls this "the mightiest power in the universe." That's a fair description of this third dimensional relationship, I'd say.

In this book I'm going to primarily refer to this third dimension as, "the baptism *with* the Holy Spirit." I realize that "baptism *in* the Holy Spirit" is also an accurate phrase from the original languages. Yet, I am choosing, for the most part, to stick with the King James term, "with," for the sake of consistency. Also, to avoid unnecessary verbiage, I will typically use the pronouns, "he, his, and him," to represent all mankind and both genders, thus avoiding the burden of using split phrases such as "him/her," and, "he/she."

In addition, I will capitalize all proper names and titles of Deity. I will not, however, in keeping with accepted styles, be concerned with capitalizing such personal pronouns as "he, his, or him." Unless, of course, they begin a new sentence.

AN ENDUEMENT OF POWER

Weekly I receive hundreds of prayer requests from Christians and non-Christians alike who have desperate needs.[9]

"Pray for my daddy to come home."

"Pray for my mother. She has cancer."

"Please pray for my twenty-one year old son. He was diagnosed with AIDS."

"I want to see my husband stop using cocaine."

"My wife of 15 years left me for another man. Pray that she'll come back to me."

"My daughter has leukemia. Please pray for a miracle."

"I am trying to raise my three children alone. My husband left me, and I'm now being evicted from my apartment because I couldn't pay. Please pray for me."

"My church is not growing. Please pray."

The list goes on and on. People need answers. They need miracles.

Christians who are marching into the third dimensional relationship with the Holy Spirit will be the ones empowered by God to bring miracle answers to humanity's deepest needs.

What about you? Are you satisfied with your life, the way it is now, or are you hungry for more? Are you content with your prayer results or would you like to see more answers? Do you long to flow in a supernatural vein and bring divine solutions and Heaven-sent miracles to hungry hearts for Jesus Christ? Do you desire a fresh anointing — a new *power* — and a radical new way of living?

If you crave a deeper, more empowering, more fruitful relationship with God, then prepare now to step into the third dimension.

"Whenever we find the presence of the Holy Spirit, we will always find the supernatural."

— *Kathryn Kuhlman*

CHAPTER 1

HOLY SPIRIT NIGHT

Do you remember the first time you ever stepped into a Full Gospel, Pentecostal, or Charismatic meeting? Do you remember what you felt like? You may have wondered in your mind, "What in the world is going on in this place?" Yet deep down in your heart something told you this was genuine.

I'm talking about when you visited a *legitimate, proper* Pentecostal church. I'll be the first to admit that I've visited some so-called Pentecostal churches that made me feel more like I was in a house of madness than a house of worship. There was no order; only confusion as people screeched in "tongues" and made strange gyrations with their bodies. I'm not talking about *that* kind of meeting. I'm talking about a genuine Pentecostal meeting where Jesus Christ is glorified and the presence of the Holy Spirit is unmistakable.

HOLY SPIRIT NIGHT

I'll always remember the night I went into Calvary Chapel in Costa Mesa, California. That's where I first met Jesus at a Monday evening Bible study. A few weeks later Howard Malone and Terry Miller, the two guys who had originally invited me to church and had introduced me to Jesus Christ, told me there was going to be a special service — Holy Spirit Night — on Tuesday.

"Would you like to go with us, Dave?" they asked.

I decided to go, so we drove 85 miles from San Diego to Costa Mesa to attend a Tuesday night meeting. As we sat in church I noticed something strange. Behind us was a group of foreigners, or at least that's what I thought. The reason I thought they were foreigners is because during the singing and worship time they were gently whispering in other languages. I thought maybe they were from Mexico or France, or someplace else. But as they spoke in such beautiful and unobtrusive ways, I kept feeling something warm on the inside of me. I had never in my life heard of the gift of tongues. But as it turned out I later learned they were *not* from another country at all. They were simply, delightfully praising God in a glorious heavenly language.

The pastor was speaking on the baptism with the Holy Spirit that night and members of the ministry team were going to lay hands on people to receive. They called it an, "enduement of power from on high," also known as, "the baptism with the Holy Spirit." Terry asked me if I wanted to go up with him to be prayed for.

"Let's go up," I bravely replied.

We walked up to the front with scores of others. The pastor's son and some of the ministers were beginning to lay hands on worshippers standing at the front of the congregation when I noticed that many people began to speak in other languages as the ministers laid hands on them and prayed over them.

People just began to speak in other languages and we didn't understand exactly what was happening. Terry and Howard both were Baptists and didn't understand what was going on anymore than I did. All three of us were open to anything more the Lord may have wanted to give us, but we were a little afraid, too. This was all new to us. Growing up, I had been a Lutheran until my rebellious teenage years. We had never been taught anything like this in our Lutheran Catechism class.

I remember when I was confirmed at the age of twelve. The pastor put his hand on me and recited these words: "Receive ye the infilling of the Holy Spirit." Do you know what happened when he spoke those words? Nothing. Nothing at all.

There was no difference in me after he spoke those words than before he said them.

But it seemed that something *was* happening at Calvary Chapel.

The lines of people who wanted prayer were two deep. Howard, Terry and I were in the second line. The ministry team was praying for the people in the first line. They hadn't yet come to us in the second line but the three of us felt like something was rising up from our bellies; some sort of excitement seemed to be trying to bubble up from our insides. We didn't relate it to the Scriptures where Jesus said, "He that believeth on me, as the Scripture hath said, out of his belly shall flow rivers of living water." The Scripture goes on to say, "But this spake he of the Spirit, which they that believe on him should receive: for the Holy Ghost was not yet given; because that Jesus was not yet glorified." [10]

Terry looked over at me and asked, "Dave, do you feel what I feel?"

"Yeah, what is it?"

He looked happy, excited and puzzled all at the same time. "I don't know but we better get out of here before we blow up or something. " So we excused ourselves and walked back to our seats without ever receiving this promised experience. In the days ahead, however, we talked about it a lot, remembering the warmth, the love, and the excitement we literally felt in our bellies that night.

Terry and I concluded that maybe God allows some people to speak in tongues just to prove their prayers are being heard. We left it at that.

A DILIGENT SEEKER

Our friend Howard took a different approach. He was a little more inquisitive and reflective than Terry and I. That night Howard went up to the roof of the Navy barracks where he was staying and peered into the sky and started worshipping the Lord. He was up there for a few hours, I guess. We didn't see him until the next day.

The next morning when we saw him, there was an uncanny new look about him. Howard loved God from the moment he was saved, but now he was glowing. There was something like a radioactive glow all around him. He seemed to have a new twinkle in his eye. There was something deeper and richer about Howard now that you just couldn't put your finger on. I remember asking, "Howard, what happened to you?"

He looked at me with a big grin and blurted it out, "I got it Dave, I got it." I probed, "What did you get?"

"I was worshipping God up on the roof last night, looking up into the heavens, thinking about God's greatness and how wonderful He is. Then I started praising Him in a language that I'd never learned. It's wonderful."

All I could say is, "Wow." Howard had stepped into the third dimensional relationship with the Holy Spirit.

I went many years as a struggling believer without this blessed experience. I didn't disbelieve, I simply didn't understand it. But I have since learned that if something is in the Bible, whether or not I understand it, I'm going to believe it, go after it, take it by faith, and go all the way with God!

> Trust in the Lord with all thine heart; and lean not unto thine own understanding. In all thy ways acknowledge him, and he shall direct thy paths.
>
> — Proverbs 3:5, 6

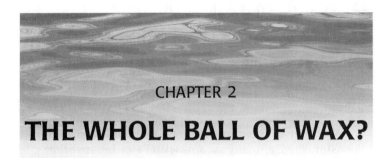

CHAPTER 2

THE WHOLE BALL OF WAX?

In Acts chapter 10, we are told of an experience in the lives of a group of Gentiles (non Jews). Up until this point, many members of the Early Church didn't believe the possibility even existed that Gentiles could be saved or filled with the Holy Spirit. They thought that Christianity was a Jewish sect exclusively. But Peter had a vision from God explaining to him that the Good News of Jesus Christ was for Gentiles also. Peter was announcing the wonderful news to a group of Gentiles when suddenly, without warning, in the midst of his sermon something strange and miraculous happened.

> While Peter yet spake these words the Holy Ghost fell on all them which heard the Word.
>
> — Acts 10:44

And this is my prayer for you, dear reader, that the Holy Ghost will fall upon you even as you read the words of this book. My prayer is that God will bring you into the reality of the third dimensional relationship with the Holy Spirit.

Notice how shocked the Jewish believers were to see that the Gentiles had received this glorious gift.

> And they of the circumcision which believed were astonished, as many as came with Peter, because that on the Gentiles also was poured out the gift of the Holy Ghost.
>
> — Acts 10:45

The Jewish believers were shocked that the Holy Spirit was poured out upon the Gentiles. Look at this next verse carefully. *How did they know the Gentiles had received the infilling of the Holy Spirit?* They knew because the Gentiles began to speak in tongues.

> For they heard them speak with tongues, and magnify God.
>
> — Acts 10:46

WHAT IS "TONGUES"?

The word "tongues," in the Greek language is "glossolalia," which means languages never learned by the speaker. It is not "dialektos," which means languages that have been learned intellectually. For example, my "dialektos" is English. If I studied and practiced the French language I would be able to speak in the French dialect (or dialektos). These Gentiles were speaking in languages they never learned. They were magnifying God and they wanted to also be baptized in water. So Peter asked the question, "Can any man forbid water that these should not be baptized which have received the Holy Ghost as well as we?" He commanded them to be baptized in water and they begged Peter to stay with them for awhile, no doubt, so that he could teach them many more wonderful things about their new-found faith.

"Tongues," according to *W.E. Vine's Complete Expository Dictionary of Old and New Testament Words,* is defined as, "the supernatural gift of speaking in another language without its having been learnt." [11]

There is an amazing, third dimensional supernatural experience with the Holy Spirit available to all believers. It is an empowering event subsequent to being "born again." I know there are those who say once you are born again you get "the whole ball of wax." Some teachers, who have not rightly divided the Word of Truth, teach that salvation is the most you can get from God. They teach that once you come to Christ there is nothing more available; no spiritual gifts such as healing, tongues, or interpretation of tongues. Some teach that the only thing supernatural now days is getting eternal life by coming to Christ.

THE "WHOLE BALL OF WAX"?

I loved listening to Dr. J. Vernon McGee as he would teach the Bible on the radio.[12] I always had a tremendous amount of respect for this fine Bible teacher. But as it relates to the Holy Spirit this was one area, based upon numerous Scriptures, I believe he was in error. He taught that salvation and the baptism with the Holy Spirit were simultaneous experiences. And the dear brother would announce in his splendid, articulate southern drawl, "Friends, when you get saved, you get the whole ball of wax." He taught that when a person comes to Christ he gets everything he's ever going to get as it relates to the Holy Spirit. Don't misunderstand me, I loved listening to Dr. McGee. I just believe that in this particular area he was innocently mistaken.

And I understand why there can be confusion. The reason for a cloudy understanding of any Biblical topic is, at least in part, because we fail to "rightly divide the word of truth."

> **Study to shew thyself approved unto God, a workman that needeth not to be ashamed, rightly dividing the word of truth.**
>
> — 2 Timothy 2:15

Now what I'm going to say in the next chapter may be interpreted as being simply a matter of semantics. But it is *not* simply semantics. It is a matter of rightly dividing the Word of Truth. When we fail to handle God's Word carefully we can end up applying certain Scriptures inappropriately to unrelated matters. It's like trying to play baseball using basketball rules.

No wonder there is confusion. For example, 1 Corinthians 12:13 tells us that we were all baptized into one body by the Holy Spirit. Some do not understand that this particular Scripture is *not* talking about the baptism *with* the Holy Spirit, but the baptism *of* the Holy Spirit. It's an easy mistake to make if we only take a surface look at the Scriptures. It's not merely a matter of semantics. Let me try to help you understand this more clearly as we continue.

"Your heavenly Father is too good to be unkind and too wise to make mistakes."

— *Charles H. Spurgeon*

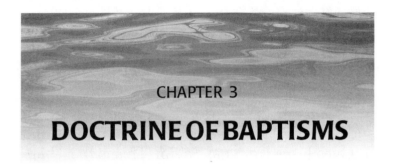

CHAPTER 3

DOCTRINE OF BAPTISMS

In the book of Hebrews we are told about six of the fundamental doctrines of the Christian faith: (1) repentance, (2) faith, (3) doctrine of baptisms, (4) laying on of hands, (5) resurrection of the dead, (6) eternal judgement. Notice in verse two of the sixth chapter it says, "of the doctrine of baptisms." The word "baptisms" is plural, not singular.

> Therefore leaving the principles of the doctrine of Christ, let us go on unto perfection; not laying again the foundation of repentance from dead works, and of faith toward God, of the doctrine of baptisms, and of laying on of hands, and of resurrection of the dead, and of eternal judgment.
>
> — Hebrews 6:1-2

THREE DISTINCTLY DIFFERENT BAPTISMS

When most of us think of the subject of baptism we think of being baptized in water, the way

John the Baptist did. That's one kind of baptism. But look, the Bible speaks of other baptisms as well. Let's find out why the writer of Hebrews used the word "baptisms" in the plural. We'll look at three distinctly different kinds of baptisms.

Baptism Number 1 — Baptism into Christ's body (the Church).

This baptism is performed *by* the Holy Spirit and takes place when a person turns from sin and receives Jesus Christ as Savior. This is the, "baptism *of* the Holy Spirit," but not the baptism *with (or in)* the Holy Spirit. This is the baptism into Christ's body – the Church.

> For by one Spirit are we all baptized into one body, whether we be Jews or Gentiles, whether we be bond or free; and have been all made to drink into one Spirit.
>
> — 1 Corinthians 12:13

Baptism Number 2 — Baptism in Water.

One of the final commands our Lord gave was, "Go ye therefore and teach all nations, baptizing them in the Name of the Father, and of the Son, and of the Holy Ghost," (Matthew 28:19). As we read through the book of Acts, we discover that it was expected of new believers that they be baptized in water as soon as possible following their conversion.

Now, the Holy Spirit doesn't baptize people in water. A minister, elder, or perhaps an evangelist or lay person will baptize the new convert in water. This is a baptism in water, administered by another human being, using the name and authority of God. This is not the baptism *with* the Holy Spirit, nor is it baptism into the body of Christ. It is *water* baptism.

Being baptized in water is a sign of true faith and repentance. It means you openly are willing to confess that you are dead to the old life and alive to the new life that Jesus Christ has given you (Mark 16:16; Matthew 28:19; Acts 2:38; 8:12, 36-39; 9:18; 16:15, 33; 18:8; 22:16; Romans 6:3-9).

Baptism Number 3 — The baptism with the Holy Spirit.

John the Baptist announced something powerful during his baptismal services.

> I indeed have baptized you with water: but he [Jesus] shall baptize you with the Holy Ghost.
>
> — Mark 1:8

The third baptism spoken about in the Scriptures is the baptism with (or in) the Holy Spirit. It is Jesus Himself who administers this baptism. This is the third dimensional relationship with the Holy Spirit.

You see, the moment a person prays to receive Jesus Christ as his Savior and Lord, something unique happens. That person is instantly and simultaneously, with salvation, baptized *by* the Holy Spirit into the body of Christ (the Church). It's a supernatural event. This is called the baptism by (or "of") the Holy Spirit. This is not the baptism *with* the Holy Spirit. The baptism *of* the Holy Spirit takes place when Jesus comes to live in a person's life. The Holy Spirit baptizes him into the family of God, the body of Christ. But the baptism into the body of Christ is not the same as the baptism *with* the Holy Spirit.

It was understood in the First Century Church that after people had been saved they could then, by faith, go further and deeper with the Lord into this glorious "third baptism" — this empowering, supernatural experience called the baptism *with* the Holy Spirit.

WHAT ABOUT THE PHRASE "ONE BAPTISM"?

"But what about the Scripture that says there is one baptism?" you may ask. "How does that square up with Hebrews 6:2 where it talks about the doctrine of baptisms (plural)?"

> *There is* one body, and one Spirit, even as ye are called in one hope of your calling; One Lord, one faith, one baptism, One God and Father of all, who *is* above all, and through all, and in you all.

— Ephesians 4:4-6

Yes, that's a good question. But, if you read Ephesians chapter four in context you'll find that it's talking about unity among believers, "forbearing one another in love," (see verses 1-3). This passage in Ephesians is obviously referring to water baptism. Do you remember in 1 Corinthians how Paul had to straighten out the believers on this very topic? Let's look.

> For it hath been declared unto me of you, my brethren, by them *which are of the house* of Chloe, that there are contentions among you. Now this I say, that every one of you saith, I am of Paul; and I of Apollos; and I of Cephas; and I of Christ. Is Christ divided? was Paul crucified for you? or were ye baptized in the name of Paul? I thank God that I baptized none of you, but Crispus and Gaius; Lest any should say that I had baptized in mine own name. And I baptized also the household of Stephanas: besides, I know not whether I baptized any other.
>
> — 1 Corinthians 1:11-16

People in the church were arguing with each other about whose method or authority of baptism was correct. Some said, "I was baptized by Apollos." Another asserted proudly, "Well, I was baptized in the correct manner by Cephas." Each group debated over which was the most spiritual way of baptizing a convert. But Paul rebuked their divisive attitudes.

Even today some people baptize in the "Name of Jesus Christ," while others baptize in the "Name of the Father, Son, and Holy Ghost." It is wrong to say one baptismal formula is invalid while the other is superior. The important thing is that converts be baptized in the authority of God regardless of who performs the ministry of water baptism, or, the exact words pronounced during the baptism. There is *one* baptism.

Let me illustrate the point. Suppose a person who had been baptized in a church that used the words, "I baptize you in the Name of Jesus Christ," later came to our church. And suppose we were accustomed to using the Trinitarian statement, "I baptize you in the Name of the Father, Son, and Holy Ghost." It would be wrong for us to force the person to be rebaptized because of the notion that our method is the only one acceptable. No, there is only one baptism. A person shouldn't have to be rebaptized every time he moves to a new city and attends a new church. This is what Paul was talking about when he referred to "one baptism." In context, he was talking about water baptism.

CESSATIONIST DOCTRINE

Someone may say, "That makes sense, but doesn't the Bible say somewhere that tongues are supposed to cease?" The reference is 1 Corinthians 13:8. Let's see what it says.

> Charity never faileth: but whether *there be* prophecies, they shall fail; whether *there be* tongues, they shall cease; whether *there be* knowledge, it shall vanish away. For we know in part, and we prophesy in

part. But when that which is perfect is come, then that which is in part shall be done away.

— 1 Corinthians 13:8-10

Tongues would only cease when prophecy and knowledge cease. Has prophecy ceased? The answer is, of course not. Has all prophecy been fulfilled? It hasn't yet. Has knowledge vanished away? No, certainly not. These things would cease only after, "that which is perfect is come."[13] This phrase in the Greek language is masculine, referring to a perfect person. It cannot refer to the canonization of the Scriptures as some profess. Any honest Greek scholar, or even Greek student, would tell you that it's impossible that, "that which is perfect," can refer to anything other than the Second Coming of Jesus Christ. In other words, tongues will not cease until Jesus comes for His Church.

Some teach that everything of a supernatural nature ceased when the Apostle John died. Strangely, however, these same teachers seem to believe that the devil still exercises supernatural power, but not God.

I know of a man who had been in pain for years from a degenerative disease. In desperation, he went to a church that believed God still heals people supernaturally. He received a miracle and started living pain free. When he told his pastor, who was a cessationist (one who believes the supernatural gifts of the Spirit have ceased), the pastor became visibly upset. He sternly commanded the man to renounce his healing because, "only the devil heals people in order to deceive them." This poor fellow. He was enjoying life without disease but his pastor convinced him that unless he renounced his healing he'd come under a satanic curse. Sadly, the man became afraid, renounced his healing, and soon the disease returned with a vengeance.

I don't understand that. Why do some believe the devil has all the power? Jesus promised that we would receive *power after* the Holy Ghost comes upon us. There is an extraordinary *power* available to every believer who steps into the third dimensional relationship with the Holy Spirit.

> But ye shall receive POWER, after that the Holy Ghost is come upon you: and ye shall be witnesses unto me both in Jerusalem, and in all Judaea, and in Samaria, and unto the uttermost part of the earth.
>
> — Acts 1:8

In the next chapter I'll relate a true story of how two women discovered the supernatural power of God through being filled with the Holy Spirit.

CHAPTER 4

THE LIGHTNING OF GOD

I think everybody has some irritating people in their lives. You just want to run when you see these folks coming your way. Such was the case of Mary Ann and Sonja.

Mary Ann, a wealthy businesswoman, visited our church one Sunday morning. She cornered me after the service, wanting to tell me something.

"Pastor, my name is Mary Ann. Please look in the offering when you can. You'll find that I wrote a check for $1000. I enjoyed your service and would like you and your family to come to my house for dinner," she announced.

"Well, it's nice to meet you, Mary Ann. I appreciate your thoughtfulness, but we're about nine years behind on our dinner appointments now, so, I'll have to decline the invitation," I told her.

At that point she seemed to become upset. It was as if she assumed she could buy time with the pastor by putting in a good offering. She huffed away. I thought I would never see her again. After being in the ministry awhile you get to know the types that come and go.

But next Sunday there sat Mary Ann. This time she had a sidekick with her named Sonja. They were right in the front row and seemed to thoroughly love the singing, preaching, and special music. When I gave an invitation to accept Christ, both responded. Later they told me that they both had a previous church background.

Mary Ann was the former wife of a traditional church pastor, and Sonja had been a member of a denomination that believes that speaking in tongues is a work of the devil. Mary Ann was divorced and hadn't been to church in a long time. It had been many years since Sonja had been in church too. I was happy they recommitted their lives to Jesus but, after a few weeks, I was wishing they both would attend some other church.

THEOLOGICAL BAGGAGE

These girls had a lot of theological baggage in their minds even though it had been many years since either of them had really served the Lord. This "baggage" created a problem.

Every time we had a service I could expect to see Mary Ann and Sonja sitting right there in the front row. They seemed to be really blessed. Yet, after every service, they needed to complain about something. Typically their complaints revolved around believing in the supernatural power available to believers today. They had questions galore, especially Mary Ann. The problem was that Mary Ann was a powerful businesswoman, accustomed to having her way, and she presented herself in that manner; assertive; authoritative.

"Well, you can't really believe that God heals people today, can you?"

"This 'tongues' business is a bunch of nonsense."

"People that speak in this gibberish are just plain immature."

And the list went on ... and on ... and on.

I think I invited them to go to some other church on more than one occasion, but they kept coming back with questions and assertions about how the church ought to be run and what we should believe and not believe. It came to the point that I had to quit greeting people after the services because Mary Ann and Sonja would be lurking somewhere to nab me, dominate my time, and inform me of my theological inaccuracies.

Many nights I prayed, "Lord, do something in Mary Ann's and Sonja's lives. Please send them to a different church, Lord."

The next Sunday I was fed up with the fact that I had to hide in my own church so I could avoid these women. After the service, as was their custom, they were waiting for me. Mary Ann looked at me with an arrogant stare and aggressively stated, "I'm confused."

I couldn't believe what I did next.

I blurted out, "Well, if you're confused, then there must be sin in your life somewhere. The Bible says, 'where there is confusion, there is envy, strife, and all manner of evil works.' You must be practicing some sort of evil if you're so confused."

I know. I know. I sound like an awful pastor. Believe me, I felt like an awful pastor. In fact, whenever I'd see Mary Ann and Sonja coming toward me, I felt like running to the McDonalds restaurant near by to see if they needed a manager. Anything would be better than being a pastor if I had to tolerate people like this, and do it with a sincerely gracious attitude.

I thought my remarks did it. I thought sure these women would never come back to our church. In one way, I felt guilty for the way I had treated them. But in another way I was relieved that they'd probably find another church and another pastor somewhere and leave me alone. I was wrong.

The next Sunday they were both back again sitting in the front row. Both were smiling, singing and seemingly enjoying the service. Somehow I was able to dodge them that day but the next Wednesday night was a different story. What happened that evening I'll never forget.

THE UNFORGETTABLE WEDNESDAY NIGHT

Wednesday evening we had a couple of guest speakers in the church. We were in a special series of meetings we called, "Outpouring '84." The preachers on Wednesday were a husband and wife ministry team and both preached. The man was a teacher and his wife was an evangelist — very exhortative.

When they finished preaching they wanted to pray for the sick and for those who had not received the baptism with the Holy Spirit. Crowds pressed to the front of the worship center to be prayed for. Meanwhile, Mary Ann and Sonja just observed with their heads half cocked.

As the evangelists prayed some people began to speak in tongues. Others fell onto the floor as if a great power had struck them. The entire service was a little more demonstrative than what we were accustomed to, but I didn't see anything un-scriptural or out of order. Some folks accepted Christ, others were healed, and still others received a heavenly prayer language in which to worship God. Over all, it was a good service.

After everyone had left the building, I stayed behind to make sure I wouldn't have an encounter with my two "friends." I turned off all the lights in the building, checked the parking lot through the window — it appeared that all was clear. No trace of Mary Ann or Sonja. I breathed a sigh of relief and left the building to get to my car and hurry home.

Just as I stepped out of the building I got a sinking feeling when I heard someone yell, "Pastor Williams, we want to talk to you." To put it in Job's words, "The thing I greatly feared had come upon me." It was Mary Ann and Sonja. I thought my heart would stop. I knew they'd try to dominate at least another hour of my time and I was tired. I just wanted to drive home and go to sleep.

"We don't understand all this immaturity and foolishness we saw in church tonight. And what about that woman preacher? Isn't the Bible clear that women are not to preach in the church? Your members were acting like they were hypnotized or something. What's going on?" they griped.

"And all this talk about the baptism with the Holy Spirit. I believe when a person gets saved he gets the whole ball of wax," Mary Ann spouted. When she parroted, "the whole ball of wax," I knew instantly what teachers she had been listening to over the years. It's perplexing how such an unscriptural phrase can make its way into a person's theology.

I was growing more impatient as I listened to their complaining. Patience had always been an area of struggle for me, so the Lord was probably having a good giggle as He was lovingly teaching me through Mary Ann and Sonja.

"Speaking in tongues — it's just a bunch of infantile gibberish! I don't understand why a person should speak in tongues. That gift was only for the first century when they needed to get the Gospel to other nations. I don't see anywhere in the Bible that we should speak in tongues today," they both rambled on.

"And I should know," Mary Ann continued, "because I was a pastor's wife for a long time!"

Finally I had enough.

"Listen, ladies. I'm going to give it to you one more time. Do you have your Bibles with you? Let's open them up and see what the Bible really says about the Holy Spirit and this phenomenon of speaking in tongues."

I took them first to Luke 24:49.

> And, behold, I send the promise of my Father upon
> you: but tarry ye in the city of Jerusalem, until ye be
> endued with power from on high.
>
> — Luke 24:49

"When Jesus gave the Great Commission," I explained, "we often overlook a very critical command He gave to His followers. The disciples were believers. Christ had already died for their sins and had been raised from the dead. The price for their eternal life had been paid for by Jesus' death on the cross. In other words, they were saved!

"But apparently they didn't have the 'whole ball of wax' yet because Jesus instructed them to tarry (wait) for the promise of the Father which was the enduement of power from Heaven."

I was using one of those Bibles that has the King James Version in one column and The Living Bible in the other column. So I continued, "Let's see how the Living Bible puts this:

> And now I will send the Holy Spirit upon you just as
> I promised. Don't begin telling others yet — stay here
> in the city until the Holy Spirit comes and fills you
> with power from heaven.
>
> — Luke 24:49 TLB

"We know He was speaking to a little over 500 people when He gave them this instruction to wait, yet only 120 people obeyed and waited. That means only 4 out of 10 believers followed the command Jesus had given to wait. Then over in the first chapter of the Book of Acts we are given more revelation. Let's look at what Jesus told them just prior to His ascension into Heaven.

> And, being assembled together with *them*, commanded them that they should not depart from Jerusalem, but wait for the promise of the Father, which, *saith he*, ye have heard of me. For John truly baptized with water; but ye shall be baptized with the Holy Ghost not many days hence.
>
> — Acts 1:4-5

" Let's look at the main points carefully:

(1) Jesus told his followers to wait for the Promise of the Father. He told them not to go out and minister or try to evangelize the world until they received this special power (Luke 24:49 and Acts 1:4).

(2) John baptized with water; but Jesus would baptize with the Holy Ghost. Notice these two very distinctly different baptisms (Acts 1:5). Also take a look at what John the Baptist said three and half years earlier:

> I indeed baptize you with water unto repentance: but he that cometh after me is mightier than I, whose shoes I am not worthy to bear: he shall baptize you with the Holy Ghost, and *with* fire:
>
> — Matthew 3:11

(3) Jesus promised His followers that they would receive power only *after* the Holy Spirit had come upon them (Acts 1:8). In-

terestingly, the word 'power' in the Greek language is 'dunamis,' which is the root of our English words 'dynamic' and 'dynamo'. In other words, if you want to have power and be dynamic for God, you better wait for the baptism with the Holy Spirit.

(4) Jesus told His followers that the power given by being baptized with the Holy Spirit would make them witnesses unto the uttermost parts of the earth. They would have the power and dynamic to evangelize and set up missionary efforts all over the world."

ONLY 4 OUT OF 10 BELIEVERS OBEYED JESUS

I continued, "Out of the 500 people who had heard Jesus give the command to wait for the promise of the Father — the baptism with the Holy Spirit — only 120 bothered to obey. And do you know what? You never read about the other 380 ever again in the Bible, but the 120 turned the world upside down for Jesus Christ and His Kingdom.

"Do you remember what I said about the 4 out of 10 followers of Christ who waited like Jesus instructed? These people actually heard the words from the lips of Jesus Himself, and still didn't obey. It's no wonder you never hear about anything earth-shaking that they've accomplished for God's kingdom.

"Today the statistics are about the same. Only about 4 out of every 10 believers are really Spirit-filled. In other words 6 out of every 10 Christians don't think *this* part of the Great Commission is necessary, thus they are trying to do the work of God without the enduement of power. They are basically operating at a fraction of the power they could be.

"Now, let's look at what happened to the 120 who obeyed Jesus.

> And when the day of Pentecost was fully come, they were all with one accord in one place. And suddenly there came a sound from heaven as of a rushing mighty wind, and it filled all the house where they were sitting. And there appeared unto them cloven tongues like as of fire, and it sat upon each of them. And they were all filled with the Holy Ghost, and began to speak with other tongues, as the Spirit gave them utterance.
>
> — Acts 2:2-4

"What happened, Mary Ann, when they were filled with the Holy Spirit?" I asked.

"Well, it says they spoke in tongues. But that never happened again. It was just to get the Church going at the beginning," she snapped back.

"Okay, " I answered, "let's take a look in the Bible to see what it says there. We both agree that when the early disciples were filled with the Holy Spirit they spoke in tongues, right?"

Mary Ann and Sonja both nodded their heads in agreement.

"Then let's see if the phenomenon of tongues occurred any place else when people were baptized — or filled — with the Holy Spirit."

I took them to Acts chapter ten where the Holy Spirit fell upon Gentile believers. I asked the ladies, "What does verse 46 say?" They looked at the Scripture and recited it to me.

> For they heard them speak with tongues, and magnify God.
>
> — Acts 10:46a

"So you see, it did happen even after the Day of Pentecost when the Holy Spirit was first poured out on the first century believers," I pointed out.

"Now look at Acts, chapter 19. In his travels, St. Paul met some believers from Ephesus. After chatting with them for awhile he must have sensed something missing in these disciples' lives. So he asked them, 'Have ye received the Holy Ghost since ye believed?' Their response was, 'We have not so much as heard whether there be any Holy Ghost.'

"So Paul took immediate action. He laid his hands upon them to be filled with the Holy Spirit.

And look what happened. They spoke in tongues and prophesied."

> And when Paul had laid *his* hands upon them, the Holy Ghost came on them; and they spake with tongues, and prophesied.
>
> — Acts 19:6

"It's interesting that in all the accounts of people being filled with the Holy Spirit, the only common denominator is the speaking in tongues; languages unlearned by the speaker. Other differences were evident also. Some were filled with the Holy Spirit *after* they were baptized in water. Others were filled *before* they were baptized in water. On the first occasion, tongues of fire appeared on their heads, but never again in the subsequent cases. Only *one thing* seemed to be common to all cases of people receiving the baptism with the Holy Spirit. That one thing is tongues."

"What about Paul?" one of the ladies protested. "It doesn't say that he spoke in tongues when he was filled with the Holy Spirit."

"This is a good point," I assured her. "Let's look over in Acts chapter nine to see Paul's experience. After he met Jesus Christ on the Damascus Road in a dramatic manner, Paul went blind for a short season. Now saved, he stayed in Damascus fasting until a lay person, Ananias came to pray for him. Now look what happened."

> And Ananias went his way, and entered into the house; and putting his hands on him said, Brother Saul, the Lord, *even* Jesus, that appeared unto thee in the way as thou camest, hath sent me, that thou mightest receive thy sight, and be filled with the Holy Ghost. And immediately there fell from his eyes as it had been scales: and he received sight forthwith, and arose, and was baptized.
>
> — Acts 9:17-18

"See there! Right there! It says nothing about Paul speaking in tongues. I knew it. You get everything you need the instant you are saved," Mary Ann asserted proudly.

"Mary Ann," I reasoned, "it seems to me that this Scripture tells us that there is an experience with the Holy Spirit that takes place sometime after a person is saved. Notice, Paul had been saved for three days before he received the baptism in the Holy Spirit (Acts 9:9,10 and 17, 18). It is an experience that is subsequent to salvation.

"Now, concerning Paul not speaking in tongues, take a look at 1 Corinthians 14:18.

> I thank my God, I speak with tongues more than ye all:
>
> — 1 Corinthians 14:18

"Although we're not told in the Book of Acts that Paul spoke in tongues, we are assured of the fact in his writings to the Corinthians.

"And even in Acts chapter eight when the Samaritans received the infilling of the Holy Spirit, it took place sometime *after* they were already saved. In other words, in no case in the Bible did anyone receive "the whole ball of wax" at one time.

> Now when the apostles which were at Jerusalem heard that Samaria had received the word of God, they sent unto them Peter and John: Who, when they were come down, prayed for them, that they might receive the Holy Ghost: (For as yet he was fallen upon none of them: only they were baptized in the name of the Lord Jesus.) Then laid they *their* hands on them, and they received the Holy Ghost.
>
> — Acts 8:14-17

"But it doesn't say they spoke in tongues," Sonja popped in.

"No it doesn't," I said. "You're right. But look at the next verse. An ill-motivated man wanted to buy the power to get people filled with the Holy Spirit. He of course was rebuked, but the point is this: why would he want to buy the power to lay hands on people if he didn't see something happening when the apostles laid hands on the converts? What was he seeing? We can only compare Scripture with Scripture. There was only *one* common biblical evidence that a person had been filled with the Holy Spirit and that was the ability to speak in tongues. Simon, the ill-motivated man, saw something he wanted. What was it? If we are true to all the other Scriptures we've already looked at, we have to come to the same conclusion. He saw them speaking in tongues — heavenly languages they had never learned."

As I was talking and walking through the Bible with Mary Ann and Sonja the sky became quite dark. It was much darker than usual. It seemed that the moon had completely disappeared, but I continued talking to them.

THE WRATH OF GOD?

Suddenly, without warning, a deafening nuclear-like explosion blasted thunderously no more than a hundred yards away from where we were standing. A monstrous bolt of lightning struck the light pole in our west parking lot making it look like a war zone. Immediately I surmised God's judgement was going to hit these women for the way they were talking to me and the way they were talking about the Holy Spirit. I knew if I was to survive I'd have to get away from them fast. I started to draw away from them. Actually, I think I was running away from them and they were hot on my tail. They were chasing me for protection and I was running *from* them for protection.

Finally I turned around and saw hot tears falling from their eyes and running down their frightened faces. And I heard something miraculous. Both of them were speaking in tongues. They had been listening to me even though they'd offer constant and irritating objections to almost everything

I said. And when the lightning struck no more than 100 yards from us, they started speaking in tongues real fast.

Mary Ann looked up at me with her wet eyes and face. She looked different. She looked radiant and humble.

"Pastor Dave," Mary Ann began, "Today I was in Indiana on a business trip and the things you've preached about over the past few months kept haunting me, especially about the baptism with the Holy Spirit. I couldn't shake it. Finally I looked up toward Heaven and said, 'Lord, if what Pastor Dave says is true about speaking in tongues and being filled with the Holy Spirit, You're going to have to send a bolt of lightning to convince me!'"

I sternly (yet half-jokingly) instructed her not to pray like that anymore. But I conceded that God's mercy is far greater than anything I could possibly understand.

Mary Ann and Sonja became precious, helpful, humble church members.

Mary Ann dedicated her talent to the Lord and became an anointed musician. She had always been a terrific pianist. But now she was anointed as well. Sonja became a fellowship group leader. Both remain precious to my heart to this day.

Now I must say a word or two here. Don't expect this same thing to happen to you that happened to Mary Ann and Sonja. Everybody's experience is a little different but it seems that speaking in tongues is the initial evidence every time a believer is filled with the Holy Spirit.

In the next chapter, I'll deal with the problem of trying to duplicate someone else's experience. Simply believe this experience is for you and you can have it. You don't need a lightning bolt to come crashing down to convince you. You don't need an angel to appear to you. All you need to do is act on God's Word and you can be filled to overflowing with a new power, a fresh anointing, and a new zeal for winning people to Jesus.

CHAPTER 5

WHO CAN WE BELIEVE?

An evangelist came to town years ago and was preaching about the baptism with the Holy Spirit. He was loud, sweaty, and torturously verbose. He insisted that if Christians didn't pursue this experience God just might have to do something drastic to capture their attention. Well, what happened to Mary Ann and Sonja in the parking lot was pretty drastic, I'd say. But what this evangelist said next sent chills down my spine.

"My son was not seeking God for the baptism in the Holy Ghost. He was in rebellion, running from the call of God on his life. We had prayed for the boy and warned him that something bad would happen if he didn't go after God for the Holy Ghost. And just as I prophesied, it came to pass. One night while driving his car he suddenly lost control and swerved off the road and into a ditch rolling his vehicle over and over, smashing his body into a twisted mess. But as he lie there with blood running down his body, waiting for an ambulance to arrive, he began praying in an unknown tongue. Hallelujah. We didn't know if he was going to live or if he was going to die, but glory to God, The Holy Ghost finally got a hold of the boy. It took a horrible and disfiguring car accident for that boy to begin speaking in tongues. And it may take something like that for some of you if you don't get serious about getting the Holy Ghost."

By this time I was beside myself. If I had been the pastor of that church I'm convinced I would have stopped this man before another word came out of his mouth. I have this protective nature, you see, when it comes to watching over God's family. But since I wasn't in charge, there was nothing I could do ethically to stop this evangelist from trying to scare people into receiving the baptism with the Holy Spirit (what he called "getting the Holy Ghost,") and this beautiful prayer language of the Spirit called "tongues."

I watched as people filed down to the altar area for prayer. Some appeared frightened. Others looked terrorized, fearing for their lives. But the evangelist kept hollering on.

"Friends, if you don't have the Holy Ghost, you better get down here and get it or you never know what God might do to you. Will it take a serious disease to make you speak in tongues? Will it take a life threatening accident, like it did for my son? What will it take to convince you?"

MY PENETRATING THOUGHTS

By this time I had developed some serious, penetrating, questioning thoughts. First, I wished he'd get his terminology correct. Every believer has the Holy Ghost. Yet he kept saying, "You need to get the Holy Ghost." Okay, maybe I'm picky. Maybe I am hairsplitting. After all, the Scriptures do, a couple times, refer to this experience as the "gift of the Holy Ghost." I'm not usually overly fastidious, in fact I'm quite the opposite, but when it comes to something so important, it concerns me when someone is painting the wrong public picture of this wonderful blessing of being filled with the Holy Spirit.

Second, the Holy Ghost is not an "it." The evangelist kept referring to the Holy Spirit as an "it." He is not an "it." He is a "He." He is a Person. He is God. Notice how careful Jesus was in His teaching to refer to the Holy Spirit with masculine personal pronouns.

> And I will pray the Father, and he shall give you another Comforter, that he may abide with you for ever; *Even* the Spirit of truth; whom the world cannot receive, because it seeth him not, neither knoweth him: but ye know him; for he dwelleth with you, and shall be in you. But the Comforter, *which is* the Holy Ghost, whom the Father will send in my name, he shall teach

> you all things, and bring all things to your remembrance, whatsoever I have said unto you.
>
> — John 14:16-17, 26

> Nevertheless I tell you the truth; It is expedient for you that I go away: for if I go not away, the Comforter will not come unto you; but if I depart, I will send him unto you. And when he is come, he will reprove the world of sin, and of righteousness, and of judgment.
>
> — John 16:7-8

> I have yet many things to say unto you, but ye cannot bear them now. Howbeit when he, the Spirit of truth, is come, he will guide you into all truth: for he shall not speak of himself; but whatsoever he shall hear, *that* shall he speak: and he will shew you things to come. He shall glorify me: for he shall receive of mine, and shall shew *it* unto you.
>
> — John 16:12-14

Third, God is not interested in terrorizing you into any experience that will take you deeper with Him. The Holy Spirit is the Comforter, not the Terrorist. He leads, guides, comforts, strengthens and gently prods. He doesn't force or use terror to motivate people.

But that's just what this evangelist was trying to do. I felt bad about it and determined that I would never use scare tactics to push people into a deeper, more fruitful fellowship with God. Nonetheless, I'm sure the evangelist meant well. He was not evil-intentioned. It's just that his tactics made my skin crawl.

Do you think that because this evangelist's son had a car accident and began speaking in tongues that everyone should have a car accident in order to speak in tongues? The answer is, of course not. Yet sometimes people who have received this blessing of being filled with the Holy Spirit and speaking in tongues tend to think that everyone should receive the experience the same way they did. Thus, we have many different instructions.

"You need to sit down, like they were sitting on the Day of Pentecost."

"No, you need to kneel down in reverence to God to receive."

"You need to lift your hands."

"You need to let go."

"You need to hang on."

WHO CAN WE BELIEVE?

Who are we supposed to believe? How about believing the Bible! When people in the Bible received the baptism with the Holy Spirit, evidenced by speaking in unknown tongues, there were no prescribed patterns or physical positions. Some were sitting. Some were standing. We don't even have a clue as to the position of their arms. Did they hang on or did they let go? I guess it's just a matter of what you mean by "hang on" or "let go."

The fact is, it's faith, and faith alone, that will bring you into this beautiful baptism of love. It's not a car accident or some other dreadful thing. If car accidents got people filled with the Holy Spirit, then why didn't the disciples all have car accidents (or chariot accidents?)

> Let me ask you this one question: Did you receive the Holy Spirit by trying to keep the Jewish laws? Of course not, for the Holy Spirit came upon you only after you heard about Christ and trusted him to save you.
>
> — Galatians 3:2 TLB

People often ask me about what position they should be in to receive the infilling of the Holy Spirit. I always tell them, "It doesn't matter what the position of your body is, as long as the position of your heart is right."

When Father Dennis Bennett, an Episcopal priest (now in Heaven), was filled with the Holy Spirit back in 1960, he began telling others about this wonderful blessing. Some would come to him and say, "Father, I'd like to be filled with the Holy Spirit, but in the Episcopalian way ... without the tongues." He would always respond, "There is only one way to receive the infilling of the Holy Spirit, and that is the Bible way — with the tongues." [14]

A GREEK STUDENT DISCOVERS THE TRUTH

Ken was a Baptist fellow who was attending a Church of Christ college in our town. He was taught that speaking in tongues was not a valid experience for today. Professors who taught that the supernatural things ceased when the last apostle died had indoctrinated him. He was taught that the gift of tongues was actually the skill of learning a foreign language. But, as he studied the Greek language carefully, he made a startling discovery.

"I found out that the word 'tongues' was not the same as the word 'dialektos.' The Greek word 'dialektos' means native languages or languages learned. But the word used for tongues in every case where people received the baptism with the Holy Spirit is 'glossolalia,' which is a supernatural ability to speak in another language never learned.

"When I made this startling discovery," Ken continued, "I came over to your church to see if I could learn more about it from an experiential standpoint. I'm so glad I did. Now I know I've been filled with the Holy Spirit. I have the gift of being able to worship God in a heavenly language and I'm ready to be all that God intends me to be."

Ken received the third dimensional relationship with the Holy Spirit and became a real disciple of Jesus Christ with the call of God on his life. He almost missed it but, because he took the time to dig into God's Word, he found the truth and truth set him free. And Jesus filled him with a greater power than anything in this natural world.

> And ye shall know the truth, and the truth shall make you free.
>
> — John 8:32

> Ye are of God, little children, and have overcome them: because greater is he that is in you, than he that is in the world.
>
> — 1 John 4:4

Here's the point. Since we are each individuals, our experience may be a little different when we receive the infilling of the Holy Spirit. God knew Mary Ann needed a bolt of lightning, but, her heart was clean. And, to convince Ken, God knew that it would take a study in the Greek language. God deals differently with each of us. But one thing is certain; you will have the ability to speak in unknown languages when you are filled with the Holy Spirit.

When you receive the baptism with the Holy Spirit, you will have the ability to pray in a supernatural language. That's the way the apostles knew when someone was filled, and that's the way we know today (Acts 10:45,46; 19:6).

When we prayed for my wife to receive the baptism in the Holy Spirit at my little Bible study group, long before we were married, and long before I was a pastor, she not only spoke in tongues but began to prophesy as well. She jumped up from a little kneeling pillow on the floor as the whole group prayed for her and began to say, "Thus saith the Lord, this is my Word. Believe ye this Word and it shall be well with thee . . .." Strange. That was the first time I had ever seen that happen.

The point is, don't pattern yourself after someone else's experience. Simply believe God's promise and take it by faith. Don't wait for lightning to strike before you believe. Don't expect a car accident to make you speak in tongues. Don't wait for a Greek scholar to come to your door. He may never show up. Just wait for the promise of the Father in His presence and, by faith, begin to speak in languages you have never learned, trusting the Holy Spirit to give you the utterance.

> And they were all filled with the Holy Ghost, and began to speak with other tongues, as the Spirit gave them utterance.
>
> — Acts 2:4

You need to know, however, that there are a few prerequisites to receiving this mighty baptism in the Holy Spirit.

"We still do what the apostles did when they laid hands on the Samaritans and called down the Holy Spirit on them by laying on of hands. It is expected that converts should speak with new tongues."

— St. Augustine

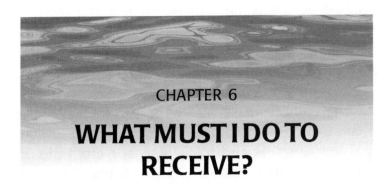

CHAPTER 6

WHAT MUST I DO TO RECEIVE?

What are the prerequisites to receiving the baptism with the Holy Spirit? Just as there are prerequisites to taking certain college courses, there are prerequisites to receiving the infilling of the Holy Spirit.

PREREQUISITES TO THE THIRD DIMENSIONAL RELATIONSHIP WITH THE HOLY SPIRIT

■ *Number 1 — You must be born again.*

Simply put, you must have turned from your sins and invited Jesus Christ to be Lord of your life. Jesus said, "Verily, verily, I say unto thee, Except a man be born again, he cannot see the Kingdom of God," (John 3:3). He went on to clarify that He was speaking of a spiritual birth.

God gave only one plan for a person to come out of darkness and into the light; one plan for forgiveness; one plan for cleansing; one plan for gaining access to Heaven. And that plan was a Man — Jesus Christ, God's eternal son. Jesus came to earth as one of us. He laid down all of Heaven's riches to become a man, show us the Father's nature, and die for our sins. He was God incarnate, conceived by the Holy Spirit, born of the Virgin Mary; He lived a sinless life and died on a Roman cross to pay for our sins and to deliver us from a life of torment, both now and eternally. He rose from the dead on the third day, gave final instructions to His disciples, ascended back to Heaven, and promised to one day return for those who love Him.

Jesus spoke of a narrow road that leads to life and a broad road that leads to destruction.

> Enter ye in at the strait gate: for wide *is* the gate, and broad *is* the way, that leadeth to destruction, and many there be which go in thereat: Because strait *is* the gate, and narrow *is* the way, which leadeth unto life, and few there be that find it.
>
> — Matthew 7:13-14

He asserted only one way to gain access to God, the Father, and that is through Jesus Christ. There is no other way or mediator between God and man. Not even religion can help a person gain favor with God. Religion, no matter how strict, ascetic, or complicated, cannot bring everlasting peace to the tormented soul. Only Jesus Christ can do that.

Jesus saith unto him, I am the way, the truth, and the life: no man cometh unto the Father, but by me.

— John 14:6

For *there is* one God, and one mediator between God and men, the man Christ Jesus;

— 1 Timothy 2:5

THE BENEVOLENT KING

There is an ancient story of a king who loved the people of his kingdom. A great depression had struck the nation and his subjects were having a difficult time making ends meet. So the king took all of his treasures and buried them on the north side of a great mountain in the kingdom. He then made this announcement to his subjects throughout the land:

> "Hear ye, hear ye! I, your king, have seen your struggles, your pain, and your suffering during this great depression and have acted to do something about it. I have buried enough treasure on *the north side of the mountain* to feed the entire nation until this depression passes. Not only is there plenty for food, but I have buried enough on *the north side of the mountain* to give wealth to every family in my kingdom. Bless you all."

As soon as people in the kingdom read or heard these words, they began to reason among themselves.

"If he buried treasure on the north side, there must also be treasure on the east side."

"If there is treasure on the north side, there must also be treasure on the west side."

"I think it's a hoax. The king would never do that. I'm staying home. Why waste my time and energy?"

"The king said the north side, but I believe he meant the south side of the mountain. Let's go!"

So, one after another, the subjects of the kingdom rewrote the king's careful instructions. Some went to the south side of the mountain. Some went to the east side or the west side. Some, thinking the king had lied, simply stayed home and didn't bother to travel to the mountain at all.

Those who went to the places the king had not instructed ended up very disappointed. They complained, "The king lied to us." But the king had not lied. In utter presumption they went to places the king had not told them to go for the treasure. Only those who went to the north side of the mountain, just as the king said, found treasure enough to feed their families and bring wealth to their struggling homes. Those who listened to the benevolent king and acted upon his words obediently, found and enjoyed the great wealth. Those who went elsewhere became embittered as they watched their families grow weaker and poorer.

ONLY ONE WAY TO HEAVEN

The point is this: Jesus offered only *one way* to gain access to His Kingdom. Millions today are trying other ways. They are running to religions, cults, philosophies and man-made spiritual systems. As a result they are growing colder, poorer, and weaker. In the end, they will not participate in the joys of Heaven because they refused God's only plan to get them there. They will instead spend eternity in the regions of the damned, being tormented forever and ever.

But those who have approached God through Jesus Christ are experiencing and enjoy the marvelous wealth of having a vital relationship with the Creator. Those who have believed and acted on the words of our King — Jesus — are those who have found the wealth of forgiveness, a new life, cleansing, eternal life and a new start now.

This is the first prerequisite to being filled with the Holy Spirit. This is your starting point. You must be a committed disciple of Jesus Christ. When you receive Jesus Christ by faith, the Holy Spirit gives you the power and privilege of becoming a son or daughter of God.

> But as many as received him, to them gave he power to become the sons of God, *even* to them that believe on his name:
>
> — John 1:12

How do you receive Jesus Christ? It's simple. God made it simple so all of us could experience it. Simply acknowledge the fact that you have sinned and violated God's laws and standards. Have you ever lied? Have you ever had thoughts of adultery or actually committed a sexual sin? Have you ever gossiped or stolen anything? Then you have sinned and must acknowledge that fact.

> For all have sinned, and come short of the glory of God;
>
> — Romans 6:23

Sin is awful because it separates us from God, our Father. It's because of this separation and our sin that Jesus died a torturous death on the cross. You must repent of your sin-life and, in Christ, turn your life around.

> I tell you, Nay: but, except ye repent, ye shall all likewise perish.
>
> — Luke 13:3

> Repent ye therefore, and be converted, that your sins may be blotted out, when the times of refreshing shall come from the presence of the Lord;
>
> — Acts 3:19

You must be willing to forsake all your evil practices. Be willing to walk away from sins that have grabbed onto you and so many others. If you are willing to turn from your sins, God will help you. He doesn't expect you to do it all by yourself.

> Let the wicked forsake his way, and the unrighteous man his thoughts: and let him return unto the Lord ... for he will abundantly pardon.
>
> — Isaiah 55:7

Next, you must believe that Jesus died for your sins and confess Him to others. When you invite Jesus Christ into your life, it's important to tell other people about it.

> For God so loved the world, that he gave his only begotten Son, that whosoever believeth in him should not perish, but have everlasting life. For God sent not his Son into the world to condemn the world; but that the world through him might be saved.
>
> — John 3:16-17

> That if thou shalt confess with thy mouth the Lord Jesus, and shalt believe in thine heart that God hath raised him from the dead, thou shalt be saved.
>
> — Romans 10:9

Finally, receive Jesus into your life.

> He came unto his own, and his own received him not. But as many as received him, to them gave he power to become the sons of God, *even* to them that believe on his name.
>
> — John 1:11-12

WILL YOU PRAY WITH ME NOW?

If you don't remember the point in your life when you wholeheartedly received Jesus Christ as your Lord, will you pray this prayer with me? If you can't remember a specific time in the past when you know you were "born-again," please pray with me. You may have been baptized as an infant, or confirmed when you were a child, as I was. But if you somehow know that if your heart were to quit beating, or if Jesus were to come for His Church, you wouldn't be ready to meet Him, pray this prayer with me now — and pray out loud:

> "Dear Lord Jesus, I acknowledge that I have sinned and fallen short of your standards. I need a Savior to save me from my sins. You said that You are the Way, the Truth and the Life and that I can come to Heaven no other way. Please forgive me of all my failures, transgressions, and all the times I've ignored Your commandments.
>
> "I believe you died on the cross for me. I believe you are the eternal Son of God. I believe You were raised from the dead, and I ask you now to come into my heart and life. Give me a home in Heaven when I leave this life, and give me a new start now.
>
> "Thank you Jesus! By faith I know that my sins are forgiven, I have a home in Heaven waiting for me, and I have a brand new start in life, beginning now. Amen."

There. That was pretty simple, huh? Now call someone on the telephone and let them know you prayed this prayer with me. If you can't think of anyone to call, just pick up the phone and call us at the Global Prayer Center. The number is 517-327-PRAY or you may call 517-321-CARE. Do it now. It's important to confess with your mouth what you now believe in your heart. When you call, ask for a free copy of my book, *The New Life ... The Start of Something Wonderful.*

That takes care of the first prerequisite to being filled with the Holy Spirit. Lets look at the second prerequisite.

■ *Number 2 — You have to really desire to be filled with the Holy Spirit.*

> What the wicked dreads will overtake him; what the righteous desire will be granted.
>
> — Proverbs 10:24 NIV

> Therefore I say unto you, What things soever ye desire, when ye pray, believe that ye receive *them*, and ye shall have *them*.
>
> — Mark 11:24

I don't know why anyone would *not* desire to be filled with the Holy Spirit. There are so many benefits attached to the experience. But I think the problem with many believers is not so much that they don't desire this blessing, but that they haven't received accurate or scriptural teaching about it.

For the first two hundred years of Church history, it was expected that converts receive the baptism with the Holy Spirit sometime after their conversion experience. But when Christianity became the state religion under Rome, it seems that the Holy Spirit slowly was pushed out of the Church and relegated to a distant heavenly post. Believers were helplessly limited to the natural energies of their flesh. Perhaps that is why we never hear about any spiritual achievements made by the 380 disciples who did not wait for the promised infilling of the Holy Spirit.

In a similar manner, the Church, without the baptism with the Holy Spirit became impotent and powerless after 200 A.D. to duplicate the supernatural works that Jesus and the early disciples performed. This is interesting in light of the fact that Jesus promised us the possibility of doing greater things than even He did while on earth. But, we would have to do it in the power of the Holy Spirit. If we ignore or do not pursue more of the Holy Spirit (who is God), then we must try to function on limited spiritual power.

> Verily, verily, I say unto you, He that believeth on me, the works that I do shall he do also; and greater *works* than these shall he do; because I go unto my Father. And whatsoever ye shall ask in my name, that will I do, that the Father may be glorified in the Son. If ye shall ask any thing in my name, I will do *it*. If ye love me, keep my commandments. And I will pray the Father, and he shall give you another Comforter, that he may abide with you for ever;
>
> — John 14:12-16

Yet, even though the Church moved into the dark ages and the Holy Spirit was all but shut completely out of the Church, there have always been pockets of believers who still received the baptism with the Holy Spirit and still experienced the phenomenon of speaking in unknown languages.

St. Augustine, for example, the noted theologian and author of the famous *City of God* wrote:

> "We still do what the apostles did when they laid hands on the Samaritans and called down the Holy Spirit on them by laying on of hands. It is expected that converts should speak with new tongues."

In *History of the Christian Church* by Philip Schaff, the author gave a considerable record of the speaking in other tongues in various revivals over a period of many centuries.

The *Encyclopedia Britannica* states that the "glossolalia" (or speaking in tongues) recurs in Christian revivals of every age, e.g. among Mendicant Friars of the Thirteenth century, among the Jansenists and early Quakers, the persecuted Protestants of the Cevennes, and the Irvingites," (Vol. 17, pages 9,10, Eleventh Edition).

Souer, in his German work entitled *History of the Christian Church* (Vol. 3, page 406), states that Martin Luther spoke in tongues!

Dr. A.B. Simpson, the founder of the Christian Missionary Alliance, made this report toward the close of his life when that great Pentecostal outpouring came:

> "We believe there can be no doubt that in many cases, remarkable outpourings of the Holy Spirit have been accomplished with genuine instances of the gift of tongues and many extraordinary manifestations. This has occurred both in our own land and in some of our foreign missions. Many of these experiences appear not only to be genuine, but are accompanied by a spirit of deep humility and soberness, and free from extravagance and error. And it is admitted that in many of the branches and States where this movement has been strongly developed and wisely directed, there has been a marked deepening of the spiritual life of our members, and an encouraging increase in their missionary zeal and liberality. It would therefore be a serious matter for any candid Christian to pass a wholesale criticism or condemnation upon such movements, or presume to limit the Holy One of Israel."

The practice of praying in a spiritual language is authentic, orthodox, fundamental, and historical.

Churches which do not forbid their members to pray in tongues (1 Corinthians 14:39) are growing today by leaps and bounds. The power of God is there!

EVANGELIST D.L. MOODY

I was reading an old book about D.L. Moody, the famous Chicago evangelist. It contains an enlightening story about the evangelist's infilling with the Holy Spirit. It seems that every week after Brother Moody would preach, a couple of smiling, gentle-hearted elderly ladies would approach him and kindly and respectfully whisper, "Brother Moody, we are praying that God will fill you with the Holy Ghost."

Moody would respond, "I already am filled with the Holy Ghost, ladies. When I accepted Jesus, I was filled, so stop praying."

Nonetheless, each week, these two precious women would repeat their words to the evangelist that they were praying for him to be filled with the Holy Spirit. They almost became a source of irritation to Moody until one day he describes how their prayers were answered.

He was sitting in a room when suddenly the presence of God came upon him in a most unusual way. In joyful ecstasy he began to praise God and utter things that no human could understand. He sensed the presence of God in a way like he never had before when, surprisingly, he began to utter words and sounds, as if they were rising from his innermost being. A wonderful love, joy and peace enveloped the famous evangelist.

The next week he walked to the pulpit and preached as he always had but something was different. Ten times more people were responding to his altars calls to receive Christ. There was an unexplainable, magnified spiritual power in his ministry now. Moody was now living in the third dimensional relationship with the Holy Spirit. It's fascinating to know that much of this great evangelist's success came after his experience of the baptism with the Holy Spirit.

I can just picture the two little ladies looking excitedly at each other in that service, saying, "Yes Sir! Brother Moody has finally been filled!"

No, the problem isn't usually a lack of desire. Rather, it's not understanding that the baptism with the Holy Spirit is an event after conversion to Christ — not simultaneous with conversion. In fact, when Paul was writing to the Ephesians he told them to, "be filled with the Spirit." If being filled with the Holy Spirit was not a blessing subsequent to conversion, why would Paul be later telling believers to be filled with the Holy Spirit? Good question.

> And be not drunk with wine, wherein is excess; but be filled with the Spirit; Speaking to yourselves in psalms and hymns and spiritual songs, singing and making melody in your heart to the Lord; Giving thanks always for all things unto God and the Father in the name of our Lord Jesus Christ; Submitting yourselves one to another in the fear of God.
>
> — Ephesians 5:18-21

"IN CASE OF CHARISMATIC ACTIVITY..."

A group of students were attending a Bible institute where "charismatic" activity, especially speaking in tongues, was strictly prohibited. In fact stickers were placed on all the phones and around the campus that read, "In case of Charismatic activity, dial . . .."

Students were encouraged to report any charismatic activity, especially speaking in tongues. I find this interesting in light of the fact that St. Paul wrote, "Forbid not to speak with tongues," (1 Corinthians 14:39).

One night a group of students from the Holy Spirit class visited a charismatic meeting as part of their research project. They expected to find gross foolishness and a deluge of demonic activity based upon what they were taught at the institute. Instead, however, they each felt the presence of God in a way they couldn't even describe. They saw Jesus Christ being worshipped and glorified in that meeting. They acknowledged supernatural things that could only be from the hand of God. So they became more inquisitive.

The students set up a Bible Study meeting with one of the church leaders. They would stay up late soaking in God's Word about the Holy Spirit. Finally, the night came when the young church leader asked the boys if they'd like to receive the baptism with the Holy Spirit. All agreed they desired to receive this blessing.

After twenty minutes of worshipping God in prayer and song, the young leader laid his hands on the boys and they all began to speak in other tongues as the Holy Spirit gave them utterance. At first they felt kind of foolish but soon realized they had a new supernatural love for people, a fresh zeal for missions and evangelism, and a deeper relationship with God Himself. They came to the conclusion that they were being taught wrong at the institute and that this experience was indeed from God, not the devil.

When they returned to their Holy Spirit class they announced to everyone what had happened during their study project.

"That is of the devil!" The professor hollered, denouncing them in front of the class.

"Well, sir, if this is of the devil, then the devil must have gotten saved," one of the students answered with a loving grin on his face, knowing the devil will never be saved.

Today, I personally know Lloyd, one of the boys from this original study group. He has a powerful call of God on his life and travels the world ministering to believers and praying for them to be filled with the Holy Spirit with the initial evidence of speaking in tongues. His ministry has changed thousands of lives and launched hundreds of evangelistic and missionary outreaches around the world.

You have to possess a desire to be filled with the Holy Spirit. And you must be born again. Those are the two prerequisites. You don't have to be Lutheran, a Presbyterian, a Catholic, a Baptist, a Nazarene, a Congregationalist, a Baptist, a Methodist, or even a Pentecostal. You *do* have to be a born-again disciple of Jesus Christ with a desire for more of God. Do you have the prerequisites?

In the next chapter, we'll study the three distinctly different relationships with the Holy Spirit.

"The Holy Spirit is the secret of the power in my life. All I have to do is surrender my life to Him."

— *Kathryn Kuhlman*

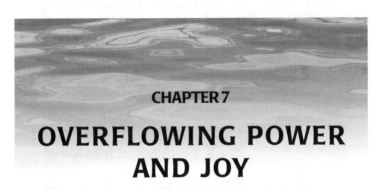

CHAPTER 7

OVERFLOWING POWER AND JOY

We need to be very careful about "rightly dividing the word of truth," (2 Timothy 2:15). Words are important. And in the New Testament there are three distinctly different words relating to our relationship with the Holy Spirit. Those words are "with," "in," and "upon." These are three clearly different words from the original Greek texts and they each have their own distinct definition.

THREE RELATIONSHIPS WITH THE HOLY SPIRIT

■ *Number 1 — The very first relationship a person has with the Holy Spirit is the "with" relationship.*

This is what I call the first dimensional relationship. The Holy Spirit is with everyone, and that includes people who have not yet given their lives to Jesus.

> Nevertheless I tell you the truth; It is expedient for you that I go away: for if I go not away, the Comforter will not come unto you; but if I depart, I will send him unto you. And when he is come, he will reprove the world of sin, and of righteousness, and of judgment: Of sin, because they believe not on me; Of righteousness, because I go to my Father, and ye see me no more; Of judgment, because the prince of this world is judged.
>
> — John 16:7-11

The Holy Spirit is the One who draws people to God. He is a great Convincer. He convinces the unbeliever that he is lost, without hope, and gently works to lead that unbeliever to faith in God's Son. The Holy Spirit is *with* the unbeliever, but not *in* the unbeliever. When you pray for your unsaved family members and friends, the Holy Spirit begins His gentle work of convicting and convincing them of their need for the Savior.

> And I will pray the Father, and he shall give you another Comforter, that he may abide with you for ever; *Even* the Spirit of truth; whom the world cannot receive, because it seeth him not, neither knoweth him: but ye know him; for he dwelleth with you, and shall be in you.
>
> — John 14:16-17

Even the disciples did not have the Holy Spirit *in* them until Jesus was raised from the dead. The disciples were operating under Old Testament principles until Christ's resurrection. In the Old Testament, prophets were moved upon by the Holy Spirit but did not have the Holy Spirit living in them perpetually. The Holy Spirit "filled" some for a season, or moved upon them as they wrote for God, yet, the Holy Spirit was not a permanent resident in their lives. However, the Holy Spirit was *with* them just as the Holy Spirit is *with* every person on the planet today.

A WONDERFUL TESTIMONY

A great example of the Holy Spirit being *with* someone is the story of Rhonda's father. Rhonda, our music pastor's wife, prayed for her father for nearly two decades but there never seemed to be any change in his life. Rhonda's dad, Jackie, was sixty-five years old, had a history of drug addiction, alcoholism, selling illegal drugs, and a host of other deeply sinful practices. It looked hopeless. But, nobody is too hopeless for the Holy Spirit, especially when there is a Spirit-filled believer praying and interceding on that person's behalf.

While driving down the road in Arkansas, on his way to make another drug deal, Jackie heard a loving voice speak to him, "I love you and I want you." It was so strong that Jackie pulled his truck off to the side of the road. Again the voice rang in his heart, "I love you and I want you." He opened the truck door and fell to the ground, uttering these words:[15]

> "Jesus, I'm sorry for all my years of sin.
> If you'll forgive me and cleanse me. I'm
> yours. Somehow I know you died for me,
> and what my girls have told me about you
> over the years is true. You died for me. You
> were raised from the dead. Oh, Jesus, I need
> a new life. Save me, Lord. Amen."

If the Holy Spirit had not been *with* Jackie during that ride to make a drug sale, he never could
have been saved and Rhonda's prayers could not
have been answered. Today Jackie is drug and al-
cohol free, and God is rebuilding his life.

Yes, the Holy Spirit is *with* your wayward child.
The Holy Spirit is *with* the alcoholic. The Holy Spirit
is *with* the sinner and the unbeliever, working to
convince them of their need for Jesus Christ. But
the Holy Spirit being *with* someone does not mean
they are saved and ready for Heaven. They only
become saved when they obey the Holy Spirit and
invite Jesus into their hearts and lives.

And how does Jesus come into a person's heart?
It's by the Holy Spirit. The Holy Spirit was *with*
Jackie during the truck ride, but, the Holy Spirit
only entered Jackie's heart after he repented and
invited Jesus to be his Lord. After that the Holy
Spirit was not only *with* Jackie but *in* him as well.
This brings us to the second relationship with the
Holy Spirit.

■ *Number 2 — The second relationship we
enjoy with the Holy Spirit is the "in" relationship.*

This is the second dimensional relationship with the Holy Spirit. When we pray to receive Christ, the Holy Spirit comes in. If He doesn't we have no hope. Remember, Paul said in Romans 8:9, "If any man have not the Spirit of Christ, he is none of his."

So, every true believer and follower of Christ has the Holy Spirit living in him. But, this does not mean they will necessarily speak in tongues. They probably won't until they are carefully taught about the experience. But, they are nonetheless sealed by the Holy Spirit and on their way to Heaven.

> And grieve not the holy Spirit of God, whereby ye are sealed unto the day of redemption.
>
> — Ephesians 4:30

So, whenever a Christian says, "I have the Holy Spirit," whether or not they speak in tongues, they are right. They have the Holy Spirit. That's how Christ came into their hearts. This does not mean they have experienced the third dimensional relationship with the Holy Spirit, but, it's true, they have the Holy Spirit in them.

I am concerned with some so-called Pentecostals who say you must speak in tongues in order to be saved. That is the same as saying that Christ's work on the cross was not enough. It is almost blasphemous. We are saved by grace through faith; it is the gift of God (Ephesians 2:8). Christ's work on the cross, and our faith in that finished work, is enough to bring us into the family of God and take us to glory when life is finished. True Pentecostals *never* say you must speak in tongues to be saved. But they will certainly encourage you to go for everything God has available for you. And that brings us to the third relationship with the Holy Spirit.

■ *Number 3 — This is what we call the "upon" relationship with the Holy Spirit.*

"Upon," is a completely different word than the words, "with," and, "in." The word "upon" in the Greek language is "hepe." This, my friend, is the intense, authoritative and *powerful* third dimensional relationship with the Holy Spirit. Now, let's look carefully at what Jesus said about the Holy Spirit baptism and how it differs from salvation.

> ...wait for the promise of the Father, which, saith he, ye have heard of me. For John truly baptized with water; but ye shall be baptized with the Holy Ghost not many days hence, ᵛ·⁸But ye shall receive power, after that the Holy Ghost has come UPON you: and ye shall be witnesses unto me both in Jerusalem, and in all Judea, and in Samaria, and unto the uttermost parts of the earth.
>
> — Acts 1:4b,5,8

Jesus made a clear distinction between the Holy Spirit being *in* a believer and the Holy Spirit being *upon* a believer. And look, He is referring to being baptized with the Holy Ghost and being given power ("dunamis" in the Greek language) to be witnesses and to evangelize the entire world.

After His Resurrection, Jesus breathed on His disciples and said, "Receive ye the Holy Ghost." At that moment, the disciples stepped out of the Old Testament relationship with the Holy Spirit and into the New Testament "in" relationship with the Holy Spirit. In other words, at that instant, the Holy Spirit came into them and they were born again. The Holy Spirit was now *in* them, just as Jesus had promised in John 14:17. But, He went on to describe yet another relational experience with the Holy Ghost, which is when the Holy Ghost would come *upon* them.

THE HOLY SPIRIT'S ANOINTING

Jesus Himself announced in Luke 4:18 and 19, "The Spirit of the Lord is *upon* me, because He hath anointed me to ....." Now, let's notice what the Holy Spirit's anointing will do when He is upon you:

1. Preach the Gospel to the poor

2. Heal the brokenhearted

3. Preach deliverance to the captives

4. Recovering of sight to the blind

5. Set at liberty them that are bruised

6. Preach the acceptable year of the Lord

This "upon" experience with the Holy Spirit gives believers the anointing to do the works of Jesus Christ. After all, we are His body in the earth (see 1 Corinthians 12:12-27 and Ephesians 4:8-16). And look at what that anointing covers:

1. Good news for the poor

2. The healing of emotional wounds

3. Getting people delivered from all kinds of bondage and entrapments of the devil

4. Physical miracles

5. Healing of hurts in people's lives

6. Powerful, prophetic preaching

AN OVERFLOWING LIFE OF POWER AND JOY

If I had an empty cup sitting in a sink with water around it, I could say that cup has water *with* it. That would be a true statement, just as it's true that every man, woman, boy and girl on earth has the Holy Spirit with them. But if I put some water in the cup, I could now say the cup has water *in* it and *with* it, just as every follower of Christ has the Holy Spirit *with* him and *in* him. But if I placed the same cup under the water faucet and turned it on full blast so that water was splashing in it, over it, around it, and out of it, I could then say that cup has water with it, in it and upon it. In other words, that cup is being baptized.

The first dimension: The Holy Spirit is *with* the unbeliever.

The second dimension: The Holy Spirit is *in* the believer.

The third dimension: The Holy Spirit is *upon* the Spirit-baptized believer.

The word "baptism" in the Greek language simply means to be totally immersed, saturated, and submersed. I don't know why different denominations argue over the method of baptizing in water. All they have to do is look up the meaning of "baptism" in the original languages of the Bible. They would have to conclude that "baptism" means only one thing; totally immersed.

Jesus told the disciples that they could become so totally immersed in the Holy Spirit that supernatural power would emanate from their lives. He promised that those who waited for this baptism would have a special dynamic that would assist them in making great Gospel achievements throughout the world.

Like a cup with water in it, every believer has the Holy Spirit *in* them. That's fundamental. Yet without a constant source of water (a symbolic term for the Holy Spirit — John 7:31), our enthusiasm, excitement, and power seems to evaporate.

It's really much like the way water in a cup would evaporate if it were not replenished. Shouldn't we keep the water pouring into us as vessels of Christ's love and grace?

A POWERFUL EXPERIENCE AFTER SALVATION

Jesus told us about this powerful miracle that *could* take place after we are saved. It's called the baptism with the Holy Spirit. That's when, like the cup under the open faucet, we get filled so full, water is splashing everywhere, even touching all the other cups and glasses around it. When you are filled with the Holy Spirit it's like turning on the heavenly faucet of supernatural power and overflowing with love, joy, peace, and other good things like gifts of the Holy Spirit. That's when we really begin to touch other people's lives for Jesus Christ. That's when we have the love of God shed abroad in our hearts for a lost world. That's when we begin to walk in the supernatural dimension of the Holy Spirit.

> And hope maketh not ashamed; because the love of God is shed abroad in our hearts by the Holy Ghost which is given unto us.
>
> — Romans 5:5

Those disciples who waited for this promise became known as those who turned the world upside down for Christ. [16] They were accused of "filling Jerusalem" with the doctrine of Jesus

Christ.[17] What happened to those who didn't wait for the Promise of the Father? What happened to the six out of ten who either didn't bother to obey this part of the Great Commission, or who swung into action without being baptized with the Holy Spirit?

What happened to those who were content to remain in the second dimensional relationship with the Holy Spirit? We don't know. But those who *did* wait to be baptized with the Holy Spirit reached the entire known world with the Good News of Jesus Christ within thirty years of Pentecost! Paul verified this in Colossians 1:5 and 6 while speaking about the message of the true Gospel, "which is come unto you *as it is in all the world;* and bringeth forth fruit." These Spirit-baptized first century believers reached the entire known world in one generation!

WHAT WE REALLY NEED TODAY

So what is it that we need today? More literature? More radio stations? More airplanes? More hospitals? More vehicles? More cassette tapes? These things are good tools for the Church, but, I believe what we really need are more believers who will receive *power* from Heaven through the baptism with the Holy Spirit.

Even today the revivals in Argentina, Korea, England, New Zealand, Australia and Africa are all spearheaded by people who are filled with the

Holy Spirit and are speaking in supernatural tongues.

When the Holy Spirit comes upon you it will be like a river of living water gushing from your innermost being (John 7:38, 39). Is this how you would describe your relationship with the Holy Spirit? Or do you instead experience a little trickle now and then? Perhaps it's time to come under that heavenly spout and be filled to overflowing; totally immersed in the Holy Spirit.

When I was attending Calvary Chapel in Costa Mesa, a musical group called "Children of the Day" wrote and sang a song about the baptism with the Holy Spirit. They sang, "You don't have to have all God wants you to have. And you don't have to be all He wants you to be."[18] The gist of the song was this: The Holy Spirit baptism can make you powerful and give you everything you need to become all God wants you to be.

If you are reading this today and have not asked God for this powerful baptism, why don't you do it today? Finish reading this book and be determined to allow the Holy Spirit to come *upon* you in a fresh, dynamic, powerful baptism. There are plenty of amazing benefits that are waiting for you on the other side of this mighty infilling.

And that's what we'll talk about next.

CHAPTER 8

TEN BIG BENEFITS

There is a deep dimension of the Holy Spirit that many Christians of all denominations are rediscovering in recent years. Since the early 1900s an especially fresh outpouring of God's Spirit became evident. It seemed to strike different areas of America and the world almost simultaneously.

In Hot Springs, Arkansas, believers of various backgrounds started coming together, realizing there must be more to the Christian experience than the day-to-day stagnant, powerless religious activities they were all involved in. They sought God and His Word to find the answers. And the answers they found! They discovered the blessed baptism with the Holy Spirit, which the Church, for some reason or another, had been ignoring for centuries. These Spirit-filled believers became known as the, "tongue-talkers," and were persecuted and ridiculed. But the "tongues movement," (as it was called in a derogatory sense by those who opposed it), began to spread. [19]

THE MODERN PENTECOSTAL MOVEMENT

Topeka, Kansas was "struck" with the Holy Ghost. Azusa Street in Los Angeles was next. Believers were rediscovering the baptism with the Holy Spirit and the miracle of speaking in tongues. The results were widespread evangelism, astounding worldwide missionary efforts, and miraculous signs and wonders.

Thousands were coming to Jesus Christ. Demons (which the nominal Church had relegated to nothing more than emotional or mental disturbances) were being cast out. Sick and diseased people were being divinely healed. Blind eyes and deaf ears were being opened. Something big started happening globally when these twentieth century believers accepted the, "upon," relationship with the Holy Spirit. It seemed that the things Jesus did while He was on earth were now being reproduced in the twentieth century. It's no wonder. Look what Jesus said in His final remarks before ascending to Heaven:

> And these signs shall follow them that believe; In my name shall they cast out devils. They shall speak with new tongues; ... they shall lay hands on the sick and they shall recover.
>
> — Mark 16:17, 18b

This fresh dimension of faith and fervor was destined to circle the globe, sweeping millions of lost souls into the Kingdom of God. These Spirit-baptized believers, these "tongue talkers," were glorifying Jesus Christ, and bringing the love and power of God to the nations just as the first century believers had (John 14:14-16; Acts 1:8). Could it be that we are now standing on the threshold of the final wave, just before the return of Christ for His Church? I believe this is a strong probability.

SOMETHING DIVINELY EMPOWERING

Today, all the great evangelistic revivals in Argentina, South Korea, Nigeria, Ivory Coast, South Africa, Australia, England, Canada, New Zealand, Central America, and other parts of the world are being led by men and women who have experienced the baptism with the Holy Spirit, and who practice praying in tongues. Some of these leaders are Baptists. Some are Pentecostal. Some are Anglican. Some are affiliated with other denominations and fellowships, but all practice the gift of praying in supernatural languages.

There must be something special and supernatural about being baptized with the Holy Spirit and having the ability to pray in a strange language. There must be something divinely empowering about being baptized with the Holy Spirit and praying in tongues. Spirit-filled believers are empowered witnesses of Jesus Christ.

In Africa alone, a newspaper reported in 1999 that, "AFRICA IS BEING SAVED." Just a short time ago, Evangelist Reinhard Bonnke, in a six-day crusade in cooperation with the local churches, led 1,400,000 souls to a clear-cut faith in Jesus Christ. This happened in Aba, Nigeria. Prior to that 1,100,000 came to Christ in Calabar.[20]

Wide public repentance erupted in Bonnke's meetings. Muslims renounced their Islamic religion and committed themselves to following Jesus Christ exclusively. Blind eyes were opened. The lame walked. Many witches and sorcerers brought their devilish artifacts, fetishes and other satanic objects for public burning. Tumors dissolved from diseased bodies. It was like the first century Church in the Book of Acts.

What is the secret to Bonnke's success? One thing for certain, he depends totally upon the Holy Spirit. He has been baptized with the Holy Spirit and prays in unknown, supernatural tongues.

WOW! LOOK AT THESE BENEFITS

Now, let's look at a sampling of the astonishing benefits of being a believer who has come into the, "upon," relationship with the Holy Spirit; the third dimensional relationship. Remember, every believer has the Holy Spirit with some access to these benefits, but Spirit-filled believers enjoy an intensified, concentrated measure of these supernatural advantages. It is much like a cup that will overflow under a steady stream of water.

■ *Number 1 — The Holy Spirit is our Teacher and Reminder.*

> But the Comforter, *which is* the Holy Ghost, whom the Father will send in my name, he shall teach you all things, and bring all things to your remembrance, whatsoever I have said unto you.
>
> — John 14:26

> Knowing this first, that no prophecy of the scripture is of any private interpretation. For the prophecy came not in old time by the will of man: but holy men of God spake *as they were* moved by the Holy Ghost.
>
> — 2 Peter 1:20-21

The Holy Spirit moved upon the prophets of old as they prophesied and wrote on behalf of God. The same Holy Spirit today moves upon our hearts to teach us and to bring to our remembrance the things we've learned. If you can't remember from week-to-week what the pastor has preached, perhaps you need a deeper touch of the Holy Spirit. The fact is, no matter how good a human teacher may be, we could learn nothing of an eternal nature without the Holy Spirit at work in our lives.

■ *Number 2 — The Holy Spirit guides us into all truth.*

> Howbeit when he, the Spirit of truth, is come, he will guide you into all truth: for he shall not speak of himself; but whatsoever he shall hear, *that* shall he speak: and he will shew you things to come. He shall glorify me: for he shall receive of mine, and shall shew *it* unto you.
>
> — John 16:13-14

> Beloved, believe not every spirit, but try the spirits whether they are of God: because many false prophets are gone out into the world. Hereby know ye the Spirit of God: Every spirit that confesseth that Jesus Christ is come in the flesh is of God: And every spirit that confesseth not that Jesus Christ is come in the flesh is not of God: and this is that *spirit* of antichrist, whereof ye have heard that it should come; and even now already is it in the world. Ye are of God, little children, and have overcome them: because greater is he that is in you, than he that is in the world. They are of the world: therefore speak they of the world, and the world heareth them. We are of God: he that knoweth God heareth us; he that is not of God heareth not us. Hereby know we the spirit of truth, and the spirit of error.
>
> — 1 John 4:1-6

Deception is rampant today. Some Christians are blown around by every wind of doctrine that comes along (Ephesians 4:14). There are many deceivers out there; vipers; false prophets; wolves in sheep's clothing (Matthew 7:13-23; 1 Timothy 4:1). Some false ministers even seem to be able to produce counterfeit miracles, leading many astray (Revelation 13:14; 2 Corinthians 11:13-15; 2 Thessalonians 2:8-10).

There has never been a time quite like this in all of history.[21] Remember, Jesus predicted that just before His return, false prophets and false messiahs would be everywhere (Matthew 24:4, 5,11,23,24). We need help in discerning what's truth. And the Holy Spirit will help us if we will, "have an ear to hear." Seven times in Revelation 2 and 3, Jesus said, "He that hath an ear, let him hear what the Spirit saith unto the churches."

We all need day-by-day guidance. We are incapable of making decisions on our own. We need the Holy Spirit's guidance into all truth.

■ *Number 3 — The Holy Spirit helps us in prayer.*

> Likewise the Spirit also helpeth our infirmities: for we know not what we should pray for as we ought: but the Spirit itself maketh intercession for us with groanings which cannot be uttered. And he that searcheth the hearts knoweth what *is* the mind of the Spirit, because he maketh intercession for the saints according to *the will of* God. And we know that all things work together for good to them that love God, to them who are the called according to *his* purpose.
>
> — Romans 8:26-28

The Holy Spirit assists us when we don't know exactly how or what to pray. We sometimes quote verse 28, "And we know that all things work together for good to them that love God, to them that are the called according to His purpose." But in reality, this promise is connected with verses 26 and 27. It's after we have prayed with "groanings which cannot be uttered" that *then* things will work together for our good.

THE SUNDAY I WOKE UP LATE

Have you ever faced situations where you just didn't know how to pray? Do you want everything to work out for your good? Then pray with the Holy Spirit.

I'm so thankful to God that I learned this early in my pastoral ministry. One weekend I was having a real struggle preparing a message for Sunday morning. Nothing seemed to be coming together. Finally, late Saturday night I put together some message that I really wasn't comfortable with, but it was all I had.

That night I felt uneasy. I began to groan in the Spirit. I was drawing a blank. My mind seemed like a bee's nest, full of buzzing and activity. I couldn't seem to hear from God that day for some reason. Maybe because I had allowed too many distractions during the week. Whatever the reason, there I lay in bed groaning. In a few hours I'd have to be up, and preaching at three Sunday morning services, and I had no real sermon stirring in my heart.

So I lay in bed groaning before the Lord. Soon I switched to my prayer language (tongues). I went to sleep praying in tongues and when I woke up, I was still praying in tongues. My wife told me I prayed in tongues throughout the night in my sleep. I looked at the clock and felt a flash of horror come over me. It was seven o'clock! I'm normally up at 4:45 a.m. on Sundays so I can have a couple hours at the church to pray before the services. "This is just great," I thought sarcastically. "I have no real sermon and now I won't even have an hour to pray before the first service."

But as I drove down the road on my seven-mile trip to the church, God spoke a word to my heart. "Now is the day of salvation." In a flash, less than 10 seconds, the Holy Spirit gave me a message to preach. I continued praying in tongues for the duration of the drive. Even as I took a quick shower in my office bathroom, I was praying in tongues and with "groanings" which could not be uttered.

SOMETHING SUPERNATURAL HAPPENED

When I stepped into the pulpit, something supernatural happened. It seemed as though the Holy Spirit was filling my mouth with words. At all three services I gave a simple invitation for people to receive Jesus Christ. There were probably a little over 3000 people in attendance, which was about normal back then. When we counted the number of converts who were now destined to become disciples for Christ, we were stunned to learn that over 300 people responded that morning to my simple, clear, no nonsense salvation invitation. At the 11:30 a.m. service, we had no more room at the altars for all the new converts, we had to bring them right up on the platform.

Normally on a Sunday morning, we will see between 35 and 60 people come to accept Jesus Christ as Lord. But that day, just an ordinary Sunday, over 300 people came to Jesus. I was glad I had prayed with groanings and tongues and allowed the Holy Spirit to help me pray during my time of weakness. This is a wonderful benefit provided by the Holy Spirit.

■ *Number 4 — The Holy Spirit helps us become more creative.*

> In the beginning God created the heaven and the earth. And the earth was without form, and void; and darkness *was* upon the face of the deep. And the Spirit of God moved upon the face of the waters.
>
> — Genesis 1:1-2

> Thou sendest forth thy spirit, they are created: and thou renewest the face of the earth.
>
> — Psalm 104:30

The Holy Spirit is God. Being God, He is the Creator. He has the unique capacity to help His people become more creative in solving problems, meeting needs, and healing hurts. Please don't see this as just a "religious" function of the Holy Spirit. The fact is, He will help you become more creative in your business, on the job, at home, as well as in your ministry.

I know of a Spirit-filled florist who prays in tongues over every flower arrangement he creates. They are one of a kind. The Holy Spirit has poured the gift of creativity into this man's life and, as a side benefit, brought massive amounts of business to this believer from customers who want something very special. It seems that his flower arrangements exude with a special anointing.

Some Christians are good at bringing problems to their pastor. But Christians who are staying in "the river" of the Holy Spirit bring solutions, not just problems. I need a stronger touch of creativity, so I need a stronger touch of the Holy Spirit. I need Him not only *with* me, and not only *in* me, but *upon* me as well.

■ *Number 5 — The Holy Spirit brings us revelation, inspiration, and illumination.*

> **But God hath revealed *them* unto us by his Spirit: for the Spirit searcheth all things, yea, the deep things of God.**
>
> **— 1 Corinthians 2:10**

We often refer to this verse as if it were speaking about Heaven. But a careful look would reveal that it is actually talking about right now. God has wonderful things prepared for your life; things that are quite beyond your human thoughts or imagination.

Wouldn't it be great to have a deeper touch of the Holy Spirit so we can gain a deeper revelation of His glorious plan for our lives?

■ *Number 6 — The Holy Spirit gives us the anointing.*

> The Spirit of the Lord *is* upon me, because he hath anointed me to preach the Gospel to the poor; he hath sent me to heal the brokenhearted, to preach deliverance to the captives, and recovering of sight to the blind, to set at liberty them that are bruised, to preach the acceptable year of the Lord.
>
> — Luke 4:18-19

> And it shall come to pass in that day, *that* his burden shall be taken away from off thy shoulder, and his yoke from off thy neck, and the yoke shall be destroyed because of the anointing.
>
> — Isaiah 10:27

> How God anointed Jesus of Nazareth with the Holy Ghost and with power: who went about doing good, and healing all that were oppressed of the devil; for God was with him.
>
> — Acts 10:38

The anointing is like a supernatural authority and power that is painted all over us. It gives us the means to achieve supernatural results. The anointing breaks yokes.

PASTOR, ARE YOU ANOINTED OR NOT?

Why is it that two preachers can preach almost identical messages in almost an identical manner, but one will impact lives and one will not? The answer is the anointing. Why is it that some ministries have great miracles and others do not? The answer is the anointing. Why is it that one counselor can counsel with a troubled individual for months with very little results, but another counselor breaks their bondage almost overnight? The answer is the anointing.

The Holy Spirit is the One who gives us the anointing.

A professor from a famous seminary was studying the church growth movement of the 1980s and made a shocking discovery. He was investigating and researching the revivals in Argentina and the phenomenal church growth that nation was experiencing. To his amazement, all the evangelism, growth, outreach and miracles were being seen in the Pentecostal churches. He came to the conclusion that the anointing of the Holy Spirit, the misunderstood practice of speaking in tongues, and being filled with the Holy Spirit were the keys to reaching the world quickly for Christ. He not only wrote a book about it but also became Spirit-filled himself. He had served Christ for decades and knew the Holy Spirit was *in* him all that time, but now the Holy Spirit is *upon* him and he is enjoying miracles in his New Testament-like ministry.

The Holy Spirit brings us anointing to achieve more than we can achieve on our own. It seems that once we receive the baptism with the Holy

Spirit, the Lord begins to work with us confirming His Word with signs following (Mark 16:20).

■ *Number 7 — The Holy Spirit assists us in our personal worship.*

> For if I pray in an *unknown* tongue, my spirit prayeth, but my understanding is unfruitful. What is it then? I will pray with the spirit, and I will pray with the understanding also: I will sing with the spirit, and I will sing with the understanding also.
>
> — 1 Corinthians 14:14-15

> Speaking to yourselves in psalms and hymns and spiritual songs, singing and making melody in your heart to the Lord; Giving thanks always for all things unto God the Father in the name of our Lord Jesus Christ;
>
> — Ephesians 5:19-20

> Let the word of Christ dwell in you richly in all wisdom; teaching and admonishing one another in psalms and hymns and spiritual songs, singing with grace in your hearts to the Lord.
>
> — Colossians 3:16

On the day of Pentecost when the first century believers were filled with the Holy Spirit, they began to speak in tongues. It says they were magnifying God in tongues. They were not preaching the Gospel in other languages and never did. They worshiped and magnified the Lord in their supernatural, unknown tongue.

Haven't you ever been overwhelmed with gratitude to God for what He's done in your life, yet you just can't seem to find the right words to say "thanks?" This is one of the chief reasons the Holy Spirit gives us a "prayer language." When we want to tell God how much we love him and how thankful we are to Him, but can't seem to say it in a satisfying way to our hearts, we can magnify Him in an unknown language given by the Holy Spirit.

■ *Number 8 — The Holy Spirit grants to us gifts and ministries.*

> But the manifestation of the Spirit is given to every man to profit withal. For to one is given by the Spirit the word of wisdom; to another the word of knowledge by the same Spirit; To another faith by the same Spirit; to another the gifts of healing by the same Spirit; to another the working of miracles; to another prophecy; to another discerning of spirits; to another *divers* kinds of tongues; to another the interpretation of tongues:
>
> — 1 Corinthians 12:7-10

The baptism with the Holy Spirit, accompanied by the initial evidence of speaking in tongues, is the gateway to all the supernatural gifts from God. Just look at the possibilities from this short listing in 1 Corinthians 12:

• *Word of wisdom.*

This is a divine fragment of God's wisdom given in a special time of need. You may face many choices that look good, but only one choice is God's choice. In that situation you need a word of wisdom.

• *Word of knowledge.*

This gift will tell you something you could know no other way. This gift will help parents in raising and protecting their children. It will help pastors to know the precise source of problems in their churches.

A pastor walked up to a man in the congregation and said, "Sir, God loves you very much. He knows you were planning to take your own life tonight and that you came here, hoping to find relief from your depression as a last resort. Well, sir, God does love you and is going to deliver you now, in the name of Jesus!"

The man began to weep as he pulled a loaded revolver out of his jeans and handed it to the preacher. How did that preacher know what the man had planned? It was the gift of a word of knowledge.

There have been times during our services that I knew the exact number of unsaved people in attendance. One night I said, "There are eighteen people here tonight who will make their peace with Jesus Christ." When I gave the altar call, eighteen weeping souls stumbled up to the altar to receive Christ.

• *Gift of faith.*

This is a supernatural faith from God Himself. This gift of faith allows us to reach beyond the natural realm and into the creative realm of God's invisible kingdom. What do you need that is just beyond your reach? The gift of faith is your answer.

• *Gifts of healing.*

This gift will bring divine healing to the sick and diseased without the aid of natural means.

• *Working of miracles.*

This gift defies all natural laws. It can bring supernatural supply in times of need, can create a new body part, a new organ, or can even cause an iron ax head to float on water. It can cause a bush to be ablaze in fire but not burn to ashes. Notice, it was after the apostles were filled with the Holy Spirit, they were able to perform wonders and signs (Acts 2:43).

• *Gift of prophecy.*

This is the anointing of the Holy Spirit to speak forth the mind of God in a given situation.

• *Discerning of spirits.*

This is your divine defense against deception. It's the ability to see motivating spirits behind people, movements, groups, or doctrines.

• *Diverse kinds of tongues.*

This is the supernatural ability to speak in languages never learned. They may be languages understood by someone, but not by the speaker. They may also be languages of angels; heavenly languages (1 Corinthians 13:1).

• *Interpretation of tongues.*

This gift is the divine ability to interpret what you or someone else has said in tongues.

The baptism with the Holy Spirit opens the door to these gifts.

■ *Number 9 — The Holy Spirit helps us develop in character and beauty.*

This I say then, Walk in the Spirit, and ye shall not fulfil the lust of the flesh. For the flesh lusteth against the Spirit, and the Spirit against the flesh: and these are contrary the one to the other: so that ye cannot do the things that ye would. But if ye be led of the Spirit, ye are not under the law. Now the works of the flesh are manifest, which are *these*; Adultery, fornication, uncleanness, lasciviousness, Idolatry, witchcraft, hatred, variance, emulations, wrath, strife, seditions, heresies, Envyings, murders, drunkenness, revellings, and such like: of the which I tell you before, as I have also told *you* in time past, that they which do such things shall not inherit the kingdom of God. But the fruit of the Spirit is love, joy, peace, longsuffering, gentleness, goodness, faith, Meekness, temperance: against such there is no law. And they that are Christ's have crucified the flesh with the affections and lusts. If we live in the Spirit, let us also walk in the Spirit.

— Galatians 5:16-25

If we obey St. Paul's admonition to be ever filled with the Holy Spirit, we will develop in our character more quickly. We will become more sensitive to the voice of the Holy Spirit when He gently convicts us of wrong attitudes, thoughts, words and actions.

I just can't live the Christian life without the assistance of the Holy Spirit. He is the One who helps me live holy, pleasing to the Father. I realize that some of those who have been baptized in the Holy Spirit and have once spoken in tongues are now living morally shabby lives. It may be that they haven't stayed under that Holy Ghost "spout." They may have enjoyed an original experience with the Holy Spirit, but since moved away from the river of living water. Or possibly, they've never really nurtured their third dimensional relationship with the Holy Spirit.

HOLY CHANGES

We'll see positive, holy changes in our lives, without hardly trying, if we'll be baptized in the Holy Spirit and stay filled with the Holy Spirit. This will bring glory to our Heavenly Father and advance our lives and ministries personally.

In fact, when we allow the sanctifying work of the Holy Spirit in our lives, we'll become more attractive and beautiful. That sounds strange, doesn't it? Yet the Bible speaks of the, "beauty of holiness," (Psalms 29:2; 96:9; 110:3).

In the book of Acts we're told that Stephen, a Spirit-baptized disciple, radiated an uncanny beauty. His face glowed with the glory of the Lord and those who saw him said that, "his face was like the face of an angel," (Acts 6:15). The Holy Spirit comes along side of us and helps us in our quest to be holy, thus making us more beautiful.

> I advise you to obey only the Holy Spirit's instructions. He will tell you where to go and what to do, and then you won't always be doing wrong things ...
>
> — Galatians 5:16 TLB

■ *Number 10 — The Holy Spirit gives us the power to be effective witnesses for Jesus Christ.*

> But ye shall receive power, after that the Holy Ghost is come upon you: and ye shall be witnesses unto me both in Jerusalem, and in all Judaea, and in Samaria, and unto the uttermost part of the earth.
>
> — Acts 1:8

After Peter was filled with the Holy Spirit and spoke with other tongues, he preached the most powerful message anyone could have ever heard (Acts 2:14-43). This was Peter, the man who had denied Jesus three times and deserted his Lord when He was arrested. But now we find a changed man. Look at the results of the new, Spirit-filled Peter. Three thousands souls were added to the Church in one day by hearing that one anointed sermon. Truly, the Holy Spirit gave Peter the promised power to be a witness for Jesus Christ.

> Then they that gladly received his word were baptized: and the same day there were added *unto them* about three thousand souls.
>
> — Acts 2:41

Look at what others said about these Spirit-filled believers:

> Saying, Did not we straitly command you that ye should not teach in this name? and, behold, YE HAVE FILLED JERUSALEM WITH YOUR DOCTRINE, and intend to bring this man's blood upon us.
>
> — Acts 5:28
> (emphasis mine)

> And when they found them not, they drew Jason and certain brethren unto the rulers of the city, crying, These that have TURNED THE WORLD UPSIDE DOWN are come hither also;
>
> — Acts 17:6
> (emphasis mine)

119

If the first century believers needed the baptism in the Holy Spirit, then so do you and I. We need to be filled with the Holy Spirit and to keep being re-filled. Then the Holy Spirit will be active in all of our appointments in life. He will help prevent many problems and help us solve many others.

Who would settle for half a cup when you can have a never-ending, overflowing supply of God's Spirit?

CHAPTER 9

TONGUES: THE BIG CONTROVERSY

The famous evangelist D.L. Moody once said, "You may as well try to see without eyes, hear without ears, or breathe without lungs as to try to live the Christian life without being filled with the Spirit."

In Moody's book, *Institute Tie,* he said that the greatest blessing next to being born again came sixteen years later when he was filled with the Holy Spirit.

R.A. Torrey, a contemporary of Moody's, wrote, "One reason why God used D.L. Moody was that he had a very definite enduement with power from on high, a very clear and definite baptism with the Holy Ghost."

Even the ultra-fundamentalist, Dr. John R. Rice, though he downplayed the value of speaking in tongues, quoted from Torrey in his *Sword of the Lord* publication, saying the baptism with the Holy Spirit "is a work of the Holy Spirit distinct from, and additional to, His regenerating work." [22]

In the book, *Moody, His Words, Work, and Wonders,* edited by Reverend W.H. Daniels, we read the words of Moody, "This gift, it strikes me, is entirely distinct and separate from conversion and assurance. God has a great many children that have no power, and the reason is, they have not the gift of the Holy Ghost for service. God doesn't seem to work with them, and I believe it is because they have not sought this gift."

STRANGE TURN FROM ORTHODOXY

Some of today's theologians have taken a strange turn from the scriptural and orthodox doctrine of the baptism with the Holy Spirit. They teach that you get everything at the point of salvation, or "regeneration," as some call it. Dr. Jack Deere, former professor at Dallas Theological Seminary and author of the book *Surprised by the Power of the Spirit,* believes there is a deliberate "conspiracy" against the supernatural. [23]

In Acts chapter eight, the church sent Peter and John to a group of new converts to pray for them to receive the baptism in the Holy Spirit. Obviously, the first Church recognized this experience as one *subsequent* to being born again.

Most people who read the New Testament carefully would come away with the conclusion that the baptism with the Holy Spirit is a distinctly different event from salvation; that you do not, in fact, get the "whole ball of wax" at conversion. The teaching that says you get everything at the time of salvation goes against the Scriptures and the historical preaching of the world's greatest soul winners like D. L. Moody, Charles Finney, Charles Spurgeon, and the Wesley Brothers.

THE BIG CONTROVERSY

The biggest controversy, however, is not *when* the baptism with the Holy Spirit occurs in a believer's life, but *what* happens when this blessing arrives. Is speaking in tongues the *initial* physical evidence of the "infilling?" Again, we have to go back to the Scriptures to get the answer. How did the apostles know when a believer was filled with the Holy Spirit?

> **For they heard them speak with tongues, and magnify God.**
>
> — Acts 10:46

Tongues! Oh no, there it is again. Many people want the baptism with the Holy Spirit, but they want it without the tongues. But that's like trying to have an airplane without wings. Or as Moody declared, "trying to see without eyes, hear without ears, or breathe without lungs."

DIVERSE KINDS OF TONGUES

Now let's look at what is meant by "diverse kinds of tongues," and perhaps we'll be able to clear up some of the confusion on the subject. Sometimes it's easier to ignore something we fear, hoping it will just go away, than to dig in and gain a satisfactory understanding of it. The topic of "tongues" is one of those things some wish would just go away.

It seems that the purpose of this gift is three-fold:

1.   As an initial sign of the baptism with the Holy Spirit

2.   As a devotional aid in our worship

3.   As a ministry-oriented gift.

These are the three different functions of this supernatural gift. Let's look at all three in a nutshell.

■ *Number 1 — Tongues as a supernatural sign*

And these SIGNS shall follow them that believe; In my name shall they cast out devils; they shall speak with new tongues;

— Mark 16:17
(emphasis mine)

Wherefore tongues are for a SIGN, not to them that believe, but to them that believe not:

— 1 Corinthians 14:22
(emphasis mine)

What sign did the first apostles look for to prove that a person had been filled with the Holy Spirit? It was tongues (Acts 2:4; 10:44-46; 19:6). If you do not believe someone is filled with the Holy Spirit, the gift of tongues is a sign. It is only an initial sign, however. Long term signs of the baptism in the Holy Spirit will be effective witnessing for Jesus Christ, a life of holiness and fruit (Galatians 5:22,23), and a ministry of power (Acts 1:8).

This supernatural *sign* appeared first on the day of Pentecost, fifty days after the resurrection of Jesus. Speaking in tongues was a *sign* that the Holy Spirit had arrived in His fullness.

A JEWISH LADY FINDS MESSIAH

In a gospel service, a Jewish lady was converted to Jesus Christ when a Gentile spoke in tongues. The language was perfect Hebrew, although the speaker did not know intellectually how to speak Hebrew. This was a *sign* from God.

BEFORE WE KILL AND EAT YOU...

H.B. Garlock, a missionary, had been tied to a stake as natives prepared to burn him to death. He began speaking in a language unknown to him, and suddenly the natives released him believing that he was sent by the "gods." Why? Garlock had unknowingly spoken *their* language and, through this miracle, was able to minister the Gospel of Jesus Christ.[24]

■ *Number 2 — Tongues as a devotional aid in prayer and worship*

> For if I pray in an *unknown* tongue, my spirit prayeth, but my understanding is unfruitful. What is it then? I will pray with the spirit, and I will pray with the understanding also: I will sing with the spirit, and I will sing with the understanding also. Else when thou shalt bless with the spirit, how shall he that occupieth the room of the unlearned say Amen at thy giving of thanks, seeing he understandeth not what thou sayest? For thou verily givest thanks well, but the other is not edified. I thank my God, I speak with tongues more than ye all:
>
> — 1 Corinthians 14:14-18

By speaking in tongues, Spirit-filled believers experience a new dimension of prayer and worship. It's a dimension where your spirit can communicate directly with God.

TONGUES IS NOT A GIFT FOR PREACHING

Notice that on the day of Pentecost they weren't preaching the Gospel in tongues; they preached in their own language. Instead, they were speaking the wonderful works of God, which was a form of praise. In the Old Testament Hebrew language it's called "hallel," or the wild praising and magnifying of God. They were so wild in their praising of God, some of the people who saw and heard them actually thought they were drunk. They were drunk all right, but not with wine; they were drunk with the Holy Spirit! That's probably why St. Paul said, "Be not drunk with wine ... but be filled with the Spirit," (Ephesians 5:18). Worship and praise in tongues is a beautiful, supernatural way to cooperate with the Holy Spirit in magnifying and thanking the Lord. This gift of tongues is a great devotional help.

■ *Number 3 — Tongues as a ministry gift.*

> For he that speaketh in an *unknown* tongue speaketh not unto men, but unto God: for no man understandeth *him;* howbeit in the spirit he speaketh mysteries. But he that prophesieth speaketh unto men *to* edification, and exhortation, and comfort. He that speaketh in an *unknown* tongue edifieth himself; but he that prophesieth edifieth the church. I would that ye all spake with tongues, but rather that ye prophesied: for greater *is* he that prophesieth than he that speaketh with tongues, except he interpret, that the church may receive edifying. Now, brethren, if I come unto you speaking with tongues, what shall I profit you, except I shall speak to you either by revelation, or by knowledge, or by prophesying, or by doctrine?
>
> —1 Corinthians 14:2-6

There are certain Spirit-filled believers whom God anoints to the public ministry of tongues. This happens when a believer, in a meeting of Christians, speaks aloud a divine utterance under the anointing of God's Spirit. This gift, listed with those in 1 Corinthians 12:8-10, is ministry oriented tongues. As shown above, there is a "kind" of tongue used in prayer and worship, and a "different kind" used in public ministry and intended to be interpreted. Even though it is all, "speaking in tongues," there are different or "diverse" uses of the gift. This type of utterance in tongues, when spoken in a public church meeting, *must* be followed by an interpretation.[25]

DEVOTIONAL GIFT OF TONGUES

Now let's look at this new dimension of prayer, focusing on the "sign" gift of tongues and the "devotional" gift of tongues. I'm not seeking to downplay or to ignore the ministry gift of tongues, but I want to focus on the gift of tongues that every Spirit-filled believer can exercise. The ministry-oriented gift of tongues is given to only select individuals, while the sign gift and devotional gift is for all Spirit-filled believers. So that's what I want to focus on here. Let's first discover what "in the Spirit" actually means.

THE SPIRITUAL LANGUAGE

Likewise the Spirit also helpeth our infirmities; for we know not what we should pray for as we ought; but the Spirit itself maketh intercession for us with groanings which cannot be uttered. And he that searcheth the hearts knoweth what is the mind of the Spirit, because he maketh intercession for the saints according to the will of God.

— Romans 8:26,27

Praying always with all prayer and supplication IN THE SPIRIT, and watching thereunto with all perseverance and supplication for all saints.

— Ephesians 6:1
(emphasis mine)

But ye, beloved, building up yourselves on your most holy faith, praying IN THE HOLY GHOST.

— Jude 20
(emphasis mine)

What is it then? I will pray WITH THE SPIRIT, and I will pray with the understanding also: I will sing WITH THE SPIRIT, and I will sing with the understanding also.

— 1 Corinthians 14:15
(emphasis mine)

WHAT DOES "IN THE SPIRIT" OR "WITH THE SPIRIT" ACTUALLY MEAN?

It's important to let Scripture interpret the Scripture.

... comparing spiritual things with spiritual.

— 1 Corinthians 2:13b

For he that speaketh in an *unknown* tongue speaketh not unto men, but unto God: for no man understandeth him, howbeit IN THE SPIRIT he speaketh mysteries.

— 1 Corinthians 14:2

Notice: A person speaking *in the Spirit* is speaking "mysteries." In other words, he is speaking something that is a mystery to his own intellect, but not a mystery to God.

> What is it then? I will pray with the spirit, and I will pray with the understanding also: I will sing with the spirit, and I will sing with the understanding also.
>
> — 1 Corinthians 14:15

Notice: Paul tells us to pray two different ways:

1. "With the Spirit."

2. "With the understanding."

It is clear that when one prays with the Spirit, he is praying without his mental understanding.

Once again let me reiterate, in the Greek language the practice of praying or speaking, "in the Spirit," is called "glossolalia," which means "speaking in languages never learned by the speaker." In other words, it means to pray in a language you don't mentally understand. It is a supernatural impartation of the Holy Spirit. That means it is part "super" and part "natural," making it supernatural.

OTHER NAMES FOR THE DEVOTIONAL GIFT OF TONGUES

This language is called by different names. Here are a few of the names for this unknown language:

1. Prayer Language

2. Heavenly Language

3. Angelic Language

4. Tongues

5. Spiritual Language

6. Glossolalia

7. Unknown Tongues

It happened on the day of Pentecost! When the Holy Spirit filled the believers, they began to praise God in a new spiritual language; one they had never learned. It's happening again today!

We are in the midst of a great, perhaps final, outpouring of the Holy Spirit. Christians from all cultures and denominations are beginning to receive this new prayer language, just as the early disciples received. They are discovering the priceless advantages of praying and worshipping in the Spirit (tongues).

As you study the New Testament and Church history, you'll discover that "speaking in tongues" (spiritual language) was considered normal Christianity.

> And they were all filled with the Holy Ghost, and began to speak with other tongues, as the Spirit gave them utterance.
>
> — Acts 2:4

> While Peter yet spake these words, the Holy Ghost
> fell on all them which heard the word. And they of
> the circumcision which believed were astonished,
> as many as came with Peter, because that on the Gen-
> tiles also was poured out the gift of the Holy Ghost.
> For they heard them speak with tongues, and mag-
> nify God.
>
> — Acts 10:44-46

> And when Paul had laid his hands upon them, the
> Holy Ghost came on them, and they spake with
> tongues, and prophesied.
>
> — Acts 19:6

St. Paul said, "I thank my God, I speak with tongues more than ye all," (1 Corinthians 14:18).

WHAT IS THE PURPOSE OF THE SPIRITUAL LANGUAGE?

■ *Number 1 — It shifts our emphasis from mental to spiritual.*

God made man as a trichotomy; a spirit with a mind and body. He intended for the spirit to rule over the mind. However, we have made a god out of the intellect — the mind. But the intellect can't bring satisfaction because we are not primarily mental creatures. We are primarily spiritual creatures.

Baal was the god of the intellect. He was the god of "mind power"! Whenever we make plans, programs or decisions based *solely* upon human reasoning and logic, we have unwittingly become Baal worshipers. Some people won't turn their lives over to Jesus Christ because they don't understand Him; they can't figure Him out. Some won't believe because they can't understand how Jesus can forgive them. You see, their god is Baal — the god of mental understanding, intellect, the mind.

But God wants us to act primarily by spirit, not by mind. God's words are "spirit," (John 6:63). When we act upon God's words, whether or not we fully understand them, we are operating by spirit instead of by mind!

God's work *must* be accomplished in the Spirit! The prayer language helps put our spirit at the top. And Christians must operate by the Spirit, in the Spirit, with the Spirit and through the Spirit. Human reasoning and logic alone are not good enough for decision making, plan making, and program designing.

■ *Number 2 — The Prayer Language, being of the Spirit, makes us aware of the Father's presence and charges us with power!*

> But if the Spirit of him that raised up Jesus from the dead dwell in you, he that raised up Christ from the dead shall also quicken your mortal bodies by his Spirit that dwelleth in you.
>
> — Romans 8:11

At our intercessory prayer meetings in Lansing, Michigan, we all praise God in our spiritual language. We bless with the Spirit (1 Corinthians 14:16), we sing in the Spirit (1 Corinthians 14:15; Colossians 3:16; Ephesians 5:17-19), and we wait upon the Father in praise.

There is such an awesome awareness of God's presence! He often speaks to us through prophecies or words of knowledge, as our offering of praise and thanksgiving goes before Him. God's heart is blessed and we are encouraged, comforted, strengthened and edified!

> He that speaketh in an unknown tongue edifieth himself.
>
> — 1 Corinthians 14:4a

The word "edify" means to "charge up" like an electrical capacitor. Using your spiritual language will charge you up! You may not feel the power, but you will know it's there by its results!

■ *Number 3 — The Spiritual Language makes us humble* (Mark 10:15-16).

It's a humbling experience to speak in a silly-sounding language (that is, it sounds silly to our educated minds). But God understands and wants us to trust Him in childlike faith to speak forth these perfect prayers and praises.

■ *Number 4 — The Spiritual Language helps us to praise, worship and thank God in a new dimension* (1 Corinthians 14:16-17; John 4:23-24).

Have you ever wanted to say "Thanks, Lord," but couldn't find enough words or the right words to express your love and gratitude to God? Well, the prayer language solves this problem perfectly.

■ *Number 5 — The Spiritual Language helps our prayer inadequacies* (Romans 8:26-27).

A skeptical, cocky army private came to the chaplain one day and said, "I'll believe in God if He'll answer a prayer. Ask your God to make me quit smoking." The chaplain laid hands on the soldier and began to pray in the spiritual language. Then an interpretation came to him concerning the mysteries he was speaking in tongues. Without hardly thinking, he opened his mouth and said, "God don't let him smoke again as long as he lives!"

Several days later the cocky private came to the chaplain with a new enthusiasm. But he wasn't so cocky anymore! He had tried to smoke so he could prove that God doesn't answer prayer, but when he lit up, he began vomiting! This same thing occurred for the next three days. Within minutes after telling the chaplain his story, the private dropped to his knees and accepted Jesus Christ as Lord and Savior.

I hope you can see the value of developing the spiritual language. It's a gift from the Holy Spirit to Christians who will ask God to fill them with the Holy Spirit (Luke 11:13).

If you will do the "natural," God will do the "super," and you will have a supernatural new prayer language. Just begin to praise God, but don't use English. Remember, it's *you* who speaks in tongues, not the Holy Spirit. He gives you the ability, but *you* must do it.

TWO BIG MYTHS EXPOSED

"You better be careful, or you might get a demon," the minister warned a young convert who had questions about speaking in tongues.

Perhaps you have heard this yourself.

MARY JO'S STORY

It happened to my wife, Mary Jo, long before she was my wife.

After she was converted at the age of twenty-one, she began looking for a Bible school to attend. She picked up the phone, dialed the number for directory assistance and asked, "Do you know of any Bible colleges?" The operator gave her a telephone number for a Bible college in Texas, so Mary Jo decided to drive out there to investigate.

You need to understand, my wife never does anything halfheartedly. When she accepted Christ she was determined to go all the way with God, no matter what it would cost. And as she pursued God with all of her heart, He filled her with the Holy Spirit at a little Bible study group I was conducting back then. Now, she wanted to get a Bible education.

Let me begin by telling you a little about Mary Jo's religious background. She was raised as a Roman Catholic but had never met Jesus in a personal way. For twenty years of her life she believed in God, but had no relationship with Him. Up until the time she stumbled into a little Church of God service in Lansing, Michigan, she had known nothing but religion without relationship. But about that time, many Catholics were being filled with the Holy Spirit . Charismatic prayer meetings were beginning at Holy Cross Catholic Church and a few other traditional churches in our town. Mary Jo's devout parents began attending the meetings and a fresh love for Jesus Christ swept over many of our Catholic friends and family members.

You see, the Holy Spirit is no respecter of persons. In other words, no matter what denomination you belong to, if there is a hunger for the things of God, you can be sure there will eventually be a filling of that hunger. That filling may lead you away from a church that has the form of godliness but denies the power of Christ. Or it may keep you right there to help others come into a fruitful relationship with Jesus Christ.

Although some local Pentecostal preachers criticized the Catholic Charismatic Movement, it was a joy for me to see the Holy Spirit moving beautifully, not only in the Charismatic and Pentecostal churches, but in some of the more traditional, historic churches as well. God was doing something, and it was evident in the lives of those who were attending these meetings.

Mary Jo had been saved only a few weeks, and already she was attending the Church of God fellowship, coming to my Bible study group, and visiting the Catholic Charismatic meetings whenever she could. In addition to all that, she was working full time and planning to attend a Bible school.

Now she was heading south. She excitedly loaded up her truck and drove all the way out to Dallas, filled with wonderful dreams and expectations.

She found the college and arranged for an interview. On the campus, however, she noticed something different. There seemed to be an unusual "feel" about the place that she just couldn't pinpoint. The students didn't seem as vibrant as the young believers back home. Mary Jo is the inquisitive type and to this very day can ask some pretty intense and probing questions. After just an hour or so on that campus, she began asking a battery of questions.

One of her questions was, "What do you believe about speaking in tongues?"

"YOU MAY GET A DEMON"

The response from each of the students sounded like a mechanical, premeditated answer.

"Yes, we believe that some people may have the gift of tongues. But you have to be very careful. If you seek this experience, you may get a demon, or you may be cursing Jesus if you speak in a language you don't understand. It can be dangerous."

Mary Jo walked away from that campus troubled, disappointed, and confused. "How could I get a demon if I'm seeking God for more of the Holy Spirit?" she wondered. "What if I curse God while speaking in tongues?" She had been savoring the joy of the Lord, but now it seemed like something was trying to take that joy away from her.

But thankfully, God intervened with a series of miracles. She found out about another Bible school in Dallas called, Christ For the Nations Institute. She asked her pastor about it, and he began to rejoice! He said he hadn't wanted to discourage her, but was very concerned about the other college she was looking into. He told her what a peace he felt about her attending Christ for the Nations Institute.

And so, next semester, she was on her way back to Dallas to attend this Spirit-filled Bible school, a school where the Holy Spirit was welcome in His fullness.

I've heard many times about Christians being warned not to get too close to any of those "tongue-talkers." People have told me of the warnings they've suffered from their pastors concerning getting too close to anything that looks Pentecostal or Charismatic.

One older Christian was reporting to every young believer who would listen, that the Charismatic Movement was an antichrist movement that would eventually usher in the beast of Revelation and the final world government. Countless men have heard warnings, "Don't go to those Full-Gospel Businessmen's meetings, or you may get a demon!" "Don't speak in tongues, or you may curse Jesus."

IS THERE ANY MERIT TO THE MODERN-DAY FEAR TACTICS?

Is there any merit to these arguments and warnings? Let's look at them one at a time.

■ *Number 1 — "Don't ask God for the baptism with the Holy Spirit or you may get a demon."*

There are various forms of this so-called "warning," but it all boils down to the same thing: not understanding the character of God. When you get a glimpse of the character and nature of God, there is no way you could even suggest that seeking Him for anything could result in getting a demon. Yet, how many tens of thousands of believers have feared the baptism with the Holy Spirit because someone has warned them about getting a demon instead of the Holy Spirit? Perhaps it was a minister who is not even born again himself, or perhaps one who merely echoed the words of a false theologian involved in the, "conspiracy against the supernatural."[26] Paul warned us of false apostles, false prophets, and even false brethren.

> For such *are* false apostles, deceitful workers, transforming themselves into the apostles of Christ. And no marvel; for Satan himself is transformed into an angel of light. Therefore *it is* no great thing if his ministers also be transformed as the ministers of righteousness; whose end shall be according to their works.
>
> — 2 Corinthians 11:13-15

It's true that some ministers actually are representatives of Satan, used by the devil to keep Christians from gaining the kind of power that brings devastation to the kingdom of darkness. But, most ministers are sincere. They are not evil-motivated. They simply don't know any better and think that they are doing you a service by warning you about something they themselves don't even understand. These dear ministers sincerely believe they are protecting you.

Let's look at this mythical warning: *"If you ask God for more of the Holy Spirit, you may get a demon."*

Does this statement have any scriptural support at all? Answer: not a shred. God's Word constantly promises wonderful blessings to those who seek the Lord. Asking God to fill you with the Holy Spirit is simply seeking to obey the Lord Jesus Christ who instructed His followers to, "wait for the promise of the Father."

In Luke, chapter eleven, we are given an account that is pertinent to our understanding of God's nature. It's almost as if Jesus was peering into the future, and seeing those who would be discouraging God's people from seeking the gift of a deeper relationship with the Holy Spirit.

> And I say unto you, Ask, and it shall be given you; seek, and ye shall find; knock, and it shall be opened unto you. For every one that asketh receiveth; and he that seeketh findeth; and to him that knocketh it shall be opened. If a son shall ask bread of any of you that is a father, will he give him a stone? or if *he ask* a fish, will he for a fish give him a serpent? Or if he shall ask an egg, will he offer him a scorpion? If ye then, being evil, know how to give good gifts unto your children: how much more shall *your* heavenly Father give the Holy Spirit to them that ask him?
>
> — Luke 11:9-13

First, let's note that Jesus was speaking to his disciples; men who were *already* believers. Second, He made these statements just prior to the religious leaders accusing him of casting out devils by the prince of demons, Beelzebub (v. 14-20). Third, these words preceded his stinging rebuke toward religious leaders who wouldn't enter into the things of God, and who worked even harder to prevent others from entering in (v. 39-54).

Sound familiar? Read the entire eleventh chapter of Luke and you'll have an amazing revelation about those who credit the things of God to demons. You'll get a glimpse of your Heavenly Father's wonderful character as you read this chapter in Luke. [27] Let's look at verses 9-13.

Jesus instructs us to *ask*. Then He tells us that everyone who asks will receive.

Jesus tells us to *seek*. Then He says that everyone who seeks shall find.

Jesus directs us to *knock*. Then He states that something will be opened unto everyone who knocks. What's he talking about? Read the next few verses.

He gives us a great lesson in the Father's love. In a nutshell, He says if you ask the Father for bread, He's not going to give you a stone. If you ask Him for fish, He's not going to give you a serpent. If earthly parents want good things for their children, how much *more* will "your Heavenly Father give the Holy Spirit to them that ask Him?" His point is clear.

If my son came to me and said, "Hey, Dad. Can I have a piece of bread?" What kind of father would I be if I went out and cut a stone to look like a piece of bread, then handed it to my son, expecting him to eat it?

Or what if my daughter asked, "Daddy, can I have some fried fish?" Suppose I answered, "Sure, honey, I'll make you some." Then I went out and captured some spiders, a wild snake, a few toads and fried them all up together and let my daughter eat them while I sat back and laughed. You'd say, "You're one sick dad."

Well, the teaching that falsely alleges you may get a demon if you ask God for more of the Holy Spirit, is, in a sense, just as sick. God is never going to allow a demon to come upon you if you are seeking Him for a deeper relationship, and seeking Him for the promised enduement of power from on high (Acts 1:4,5,8).

Nobody in all of history ever got a demon while seeking God. Nobody!

Perfect love casts out fear. So why tolerate the fear tactics of the devil? It is the devil who doesn't want you to be endued with power, not God.

That brings us to another fear tactic used to frighten believers from being filled with the fullness of the Holy Spirit and gaining the ability to speak praises to God in heavenly languages.

■ *Number 2* — *"If you speak in tongues and don't know what you're saying, you may be cursing Jesus."*

First of all, it is true that if you speak in tongues, you won't know what you are saying. "Howbeit in the spirit," Paul said, "he speaketh mysteries." That's why it takes great faith to speak in tongues.

> For he that speaketh in an *unknown* tongue speaketh not unto men, but unto God: for no man understandeth *him*; howbeit in the spirit he speaketh mysteries.
>
> — 1 Corinthians 14:2

CLEARING UP THOSE RUMORS

A rumor had surfaced in St. Paul's day that a person may be cursing Jesus while praying in tongues (in the Spirit.) Paul sought to put an end to that rumor quickly when he addressed the Corinthian Church. Here's what he said:

> Wherefore I give you to understand, that no man speaking by the Spirit of God calleth Jesus accursed: and *that* no man can say that Jesus is the Lord, but by the Holy Ghost.
>
> — 1 Corinthians 12:3

It is clear as it can be. No person speaking by the Spirit of God will — or can — ever call Jesus accursed. You would never curse Jesus. The Holy Spirit would never prompt anyone to curse Jesus. And nobody is ever going to get a demon when they ask God for a deeper dimension of the Holy Spirit. That's all very clear. Then how in the world could anyone ever think they'd curse Jesus while under the influence of the Holy Spirit?

It's just not possible.

So get rid of that spirit of fear, and run to Jesus for the infilling of the Holy Spirit.

You may not understand it all, but the Holy Spirit will guide you into all truth. Even though you may not understand it all in your mind, you must believe it in your heart. I think you know in your heart, if you've read this far, that this miraculous experience called the baptism with the Holy Spirit is for you. Go "full speed ahead" for all God offers to you.

Next, we'll take a look at how to receive the baptism with the Holy Spirit.

"Faith is like muscle which grows stronger and stronger with use."

— *J.O. Fraser*
Missionary to China

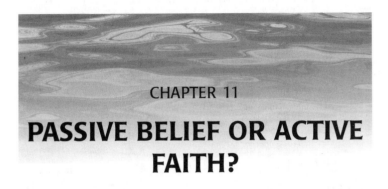

CHAPTER 11

PASSIVE BELIEF OR ACTIVE FAITH?

How does a Christian receive the baptism with the Holy Spirit? How can he come into this powerful third dimensional relationship with the Holy Spirit? It's the same way we receive everything else God has promised — by faith! Simple faith.

BY FAITH OR BY WORKS?

Paul asked the Galatians a piercing question. The Galatians were a group of Christians who swerved away from simple faith and moved into the frustrating life of human efforts. These believers started out in the Spirit, but soon added all kinds of human conditions upon others who desired the things of God.

> This only would I learn of you, Received ye the Spirit
> by the works of the law, or by the hearing of faith?
> Are ye so foolish? having begun in the Spirit, are ye
> now made perfect by the flesh? Have ye suffered so
> many things in vain? if *it be* yet in vain. He therefore
> that ministereth to you the Spirit, and worketh
> miracles among you, *doeth he it* by the works of the
> law, or by the hearing of faith? Even as Abraham
> believed God, and it was accounted to him for righ-
> teousness. Know ye therefore that they which are of
> faith, the same are the children of Abraham.
>
> — Galatians 3:2-7

Paul asks the question of the Galatians, to which the answer is obvious. "Received ye the Spirit by the works of the law, or by the hearing of faith?" It is by faith, of course.

And faith is simple. All it requires is to believe the promises of God and to *act* on those promises. Faith without a corresponding action is dead (James 2:26). You can say you believe something, but if you don't act on it, it will not profit you at all.

DOCTRINE WITHOUT EXPERIENCE

You may say, "I believe in the doctrine of the baptism with the Holy Spirit." But I ask, "Have you received the baptism with the Holy Spirit?" That is the real question.

Doctrine without experience is nothing but dead religion.

Who also hath made us able ministers of the new testament; not of the letter, but of the spirit: for the letter killeth, but the spirit giveth life.

➡ —2 Corinthians 3:6

Doctrine, when it becomes experience, brings spiritual life. Doctrine is good. Yet it is meant not only to be studied, but to be believed and experienced.

For example, you can *believe* the doctrine of being "born again," [28] but if you've never experienced being "born again," that doctrine is lifeless and does you no good at all. You can *believe* the doctrine of the baptism with the Holy Spirit, but if you've never experienced it, what good has it done for you? You may *believe* in the doctrine of divine healing, but if you stay sick and diseased, that doctrine becomes nothing more than dry ink on a piece of paper. It hasn't helped you.

That's what Paul meant when he said, "the letter (doctrine without experience) killeth, but the spirit (doctrine experienced) giveth life." Faith is what causes doctrine to come alive and be made real in our lives.

PASSIVE BELIEF vs. ACTIVE FAITH

Now, let me illustrate this principle. I have often heard people say, "Well, I believe in being filled with the Holy Spirit and even speaking in tongues like they did in the Bible. But if God wants to fill me, He can just go ahead and do it." This statement exhibits a passive human belief in something God has promised, but shows no sign of active faith in *pursuing* what God has promised.

When I finally realized the value of being filled with the Holy Spirit and speaking in a heavenly prayer language, I had it all wrong at first. I asked God to fill me and there I stood, my mouth open, waiting for something supernatural to come out. Well, it didn't and it never will with that kind of passive belief. True faith requires a corresponding action.

I have even heard people say, "If God wants to save me, He can come down and do it." Well, He won't come down and do it. He already came down and paid for your salvation and promised that He would in no wise deny you, if you would simply come to Him, confess Jesus before men, declare Him as Lord, and believe that God raised Him from the dead. You must respond, in faith, by following God's instructions for gaining eternal life.

The same is true with every promise of God. To realize the promises of God in your life, it requires faith *plus* action.

Peter said, concerning both the gift of salvation and the gift of the Holy Ghost, *"The promise is unto you, and to your children, and to all that are afar off* . . .." [29] This means that *both* salvation *and* the baptism with the Holy Spirit are wrapped up in a perpetual promise from God for every generation, not just for those who were present on the day of Pentecost when the Holy Spirit was first poured out.

What does this all mean? It means this: If you really believe Jesus is available to fill you with the Holy Spirit, causing you to bubble over with the fire of enthusiasm, and the anointing of power, then *there is something you have to do.* You have to step into the river, so to speak. You must, by faith *and* action, begin to praise God in a language you've never learned, trusting that it's the Holy Spirit giving you the utterance.

SOME WILD "TESTIMONIES"

Years ago, I had a terrible time understanding this. I think it was because I had heard so many outrageous stories about the baptism with the Holy Spirit. It almost scared me. People would give me their wild testimonies about being filled with the Spirit, and I'd sit there and listen, getting more frightened by the minute.

One lady spoke to me with a shaky, almost falsetto kind of voice, "When God filled me with the Holy Ghost, I was in the grocery store when it struck me. I started speaking in unknown tongues, went into a trance, and knocked three display racks over before I passed out. Cans were rolling every-where. It was so glorious!"

"Glorious?" I thought. "That's not glorious; that's weird." I wondered why God would do that to her. The lady gave me the impression that speaking in tongues was an uncontrollable occurrence. I learned that this is simply not true. God doesn't take away a person's control. In fact, part of the fruit of the Spirit is temperance or "self-control."

Another testimony I heard was that of a man who boasted, "I was riding a city bus when the baptism with the Holy Spirit whacked me. Halle-lujah! I started speaking in tongues, glory to God, and couldn't stop for nine days. Hallelujah! I just rode the city buses around, glory to God, speaking in tongues until I was finally thrown off and ar-rested. Hallelujah! They thought I was drunk. Hal-lelujah! Glory to God!"

After hearing a few of these far out testimo-nies, I was almost afraid to go to work. I feared that God would fill me while I was working on the control board at the electric company. I could en-vision myself beginning to hysterically speak in tongues and start to uncontrollably turn knobs and push buttons. I could see myself accidentally shut-ting down all the electrical power for the entire city. I prayed, "Oh, God, please don't fill me at work."

I wanted to be filled with the Holy Spirit. I just didn't want to be filled in the way these people were telling me it happened to them. I noticed something strangely common in all these outrageous testimonies. The people always suggested that they were completely out of control. It was almost as if they were saying, "you will never know when the Lord might decide to baptize you with the Holy Spirit. At the most unexpected moment the Lord could begin to shove a supernatural language out of your mouth." That seemed almost ghastly to me, but, on the other hand, I was fairly naive and quite ignorant about the Holy Spirit and His dealings with people.

I remember telling the Lord He could fill me *while I was at home* if He wanted. I made it clear to the Lord. I wanted to be filled with the Holy Spirit, but I wanted it to happen while I was home, not at work or in public.

Then, I felt guilty, like maybe I was limiting God. I finally submitted and prayed, "Lord, I am Yours. You can fill me anywhere and anytime You desire." It was a scary prayer, but I thought I'd take a chance.

Thankfully, nothing ever happened at work or while I was driving or shopping for groceries. In fact, nothing happened anyplace. I was operating in passive belief, not active faith. Nothing would ever happen as long as I was passive. Faith, if it is to bring results, must be action oriented and firmly planted in the promises of God.

MY SEARCH CONTINUED

I started asking more people about the baptism with the Holy Spirit. I had lived nearly four years as a defeated believer with no power, but now I wanted more. I couldn't live like this anymore. I was now back in Michigan, over 2400 miles away from Calvary Chapel, and I just couldn't find another church like it anywhere. I attended a couple of denominational churches and found no real life there. I visited a church that was labeled "Pentecostal," and it almost made we want to run away, it was so scary. I finally settled into a small, Spirit-filled Evangelical Methodist church. It was quite a bit more demonstrative than I would have preferred, but I liked the pastor, and the people seemed sincerely full of love. So I started asking questions about the baptism with the Holy Spirit.

BIG BLOCK LETTERS?

One lady shared her experience with me. "When I asked God to fill me with the Holy Spirit," she said, " I saw big block letters flying across my mind. I just spoke them out as I saw them, and I knew God had filled me. I've been speaking those words ever since."

"Okay, that's what I'll do," I thought. "I'll ask God to fill me with His Spirit and I'll wait for big block letters to pass through my mind and I'll speak them." So I prayed and waited. I didn't fully understand that the baptism with the Holy Spirit and speaking in unknown tongues was an experience of the spirit, not the mind. If you strain your mind long enough, you'll think you're seeing something. And that's what happened to me. I was basing my faith on this lady's experience instead of God's Word. I prayed and waited, and prayed and waited some more. Then I thought I saw something in my mind. I thought I saw some letters go by. "ELIE."

There it was. A word in tongues, I thought. So I spoke it, "ELIE." I said it and thought, "There has to be more than just, "ELIE." So I took a pencil and paper and wrote down the word, "ELIE," so I wouldn't forget it.

This all sounds so foolish now, but I was very young in the things of God at that time. I waited for more and thought I saw, "OLLIE," go floating by, so I spoke it, coupled with the, "ELIE." Now it was, "ELIE-OLLIE." So I wrote down the new word and waited for more.

Somehow this didn't seem right, but I kept at it based upon the lady's testimony.

Soon, I thought I saw another word in my mind. This time it was, "ONNO." Now I had three words in tongues, or so I thought. I spoke them together, "ELIE-OLLIE-ONNO." Again I wrote down my new word so I wouldn't forget it. (I almost feel embarrassed telling you this, but maybe it will help you. And if you are laughing right now, please don't feel bad. I'm also laughing as I write this).

That was it. So for the next few days I prayed in "tongues," or so I assumed, but something just didn't seem right. There was no river of living water. I didn't seem to have any more power in my life. But I reasoned that maybe I'd have to speak the words a long time before the joy and power would arrive. So I'd walk around saying, "ELIE-OLLIE-ONNO." "ELIE-OLLIE-ONNO."

"THIS CAN'T BE THE THIRD DIMENSIONAL RELATIONSHIP WITH THE HOLY SPIRIT"

Well, after a few days, I concluded *this can't be* the baptism with the Holy Spirit. *This can't be* the biblical gift of tongues. So I invited a few Spirit-filled believers over to my house to pray with me. I asked them to pray that I would receive the baptism with the Holy Ghost. They arrived and began to pray. They instructed me to pray in another language; not my native English. So as we were praying, the only language I knew that wasn't English was, "ELIE-OLLIE-ONNO." So here I went again, "ELIE-OLLIE-ONNO." Over and over again I would repeat it.

One of the ladies jumped up and said, "That's it, brother! You got it! You are speaking in tongues!"

"I am?" I questioned.

"Yes, that's it," they all assured me. But something was missing inside of me. It just didn't seem supernatural. Yet, for the next couple weeks I often repeated my new-found phrases. I didn't feel satisfied or filled at all, so finally, I asked a Pentecostal minister if he'd pray with me to receive the infilling of the Holy Spirit. He was happy to come over to my house and pray with me.

ANOTHER COUNTERFEIT EXPERIENCE

He said, "Brother Dave, get on your knees, lift your hands to Heaven, and start saying 'Hallelujah' as many times as you can. Say it at least a hundred times."

Submissively, I got on my knees, lifted up my hands, and started saying, "Hallelujah, hallelujah, hallelujah, hallelujah, hallelujah, hallelujah, hallelujah, hallelujah, hallelujah, hallelujah, hallelujah, hallelujah, hallelujah. . .."

Suddenly the minister pinched my throat and started wiggling it while I was repeating the word "Hallelujah." As he wiggled my throat, my "hallelujahs" became "wiggle-waggly," like when you speak into a moving fan. It was sort of a vibrating, mixed up sound. "Ha-lel-lel-lel-lu-lu-lu-lu-ha-yahhhhhhhh."

Again I heard the familiar words, "There it is, brother!"

"What?" I thought. "There it is? You mean that's it? Speaking in tongues is when you say 'Hallelujah" while wiggling your throat?"

I thanked him. We had a time of fellowship and guitar playing, then he left rejoicing that "Brother Dave got it."

But Brother Dave didn't get any rivers of living water. I didn't sense an unusual presence of joy and power. Something was not right. I wondered what the problem could be? So I kept searching.

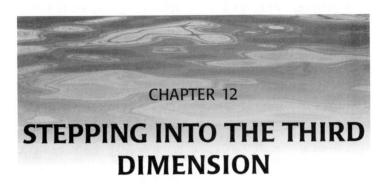

CHAPTER 12

STEPPING INTO THE THIRD DIMENSION

I knew something was wrong. Why was I not experiencing a river of living water, like Jesus promised in John 7:38? Why did I not receive the supernatural power to be an effective witness for Jesus Christ as He promised in Acts 1:8? What was my problem?

WAS I AN UNCLEAN VESSEL?

I heard about an evangelist that would be speaking on the Holy Spirit in a city not too far from where I lived. So I drove nineteen miles to hear the man. He was fairly articulate, but he kept saying the Holy Spirit will not fill an unclean vessel. I figured my problem was that I had not repented of all my sins.

THE DEVIL CAN SPEAK IN KING JAMES

I retreated to my bedroom for more prayer. I asked the Lord to reveal any unconfessed sin in my life, so that I could deal with it and be filled with the Holy Spirit. Soon, I thought I heard a voice speaking in King James. "My son, thou hast many sins thou hast not made right. Dost thou not remember when thou wast twelve years old and you tookest soda bottles from behind-eth the store and cashedeth them in for money inside the same store, and then bought-eth some candy?"

Oh, yes, I remembered this sin of my youth. I hadn't thought about it in thirteen years. But I quickly jumped up and sent some money to the old neighborhood convenience store to atone for my youthful sins. Afterward I rushed back to the bedroom to pray and receive. But again, another sin popped into my mind. I confessed and repented. When I did, more sins would come to mind, until I was flooded with thoughts of all the sins I had ever committed. I started repenting for things I didn't even know whether or not I had done, just in case. I kept hearing the evangelist's words ringing in my mind, "God will not fill an unclean vessel."

I was frustrated. Of course, I didn't realize that the devil sometimes talks in "King James language" in order to sound holy, with the purpose to deceive you into thinking it's God speaking. It seemed the more I'd try to receive the baptism with the Holy Spirit, the more ancient sins would come to my mind. Some of them, I could do nothing about, because I couldn't even find the people I had offended or hurt. It was a no-win situation.

STREAMS OF HOPE IN THE DESERT OF MY DESPAIR

Thank God for Chuck Smith and Dennis and Rita Bennett. I had saved some money and ordered an entire set of tapes on the Holy Spirit from Pastor Chuck.[30] I went to the Christian bookstore and found a book by Father Dennis and Rita Bennett called, *The Holy Spirit and You.*[31] I started listening to Chuck's tapes and reading Dennis and Rita Bennett's book.

Both the tapes and the book were refreshing, like water to my thirsty soul. They were like streams in my desert. I devoured every word these men had to say. In the process, I learned that the Holy Spirit doesn't make you do weird things that will embarrass you, as others had taught me. I learned that it is the devil who tries to keep you from receiving the baptism with the Holy Ghost, not God. It's the devil that gives you a myriad of reasons why you can't be filled with God's Spirit. I learned that all my sins were gone because of the Blood of Jesus. He died on the cross, once and for all, and His work at Calvary was enough to take care of all my sins, real or imagined. I realized I had been totally forgiven and no longer had to worry about sins I had committed ten or fifteen years ago. I made restitution wherever I could, but in situations where it was impossible, God didn't expect me to do what I could not.

I basked in Chuck's wonderful teachings on the Holy Spirit. I devoured Father Bennett's book, which is a classic today. I excitedly looked up all the Scripture references, and a fire was beginning to ignite in my spirit. I began to realize that I didn't have to be holy or perfect from a practical standpoint to receive the baptism with the Holy Spirit, for it is the Holy Spirit who would give me the power to be holy. I understood that the Holy Spirit wasn't going to throw me into some outrageous trance and force me to do things against my will and better judgement.

Listening to those tapes and reading that book was like getting a whole new concept of the greatness of God and His love for me. I was no longer afraid of God striking me with the Holy Ghost in some awkward moment. This was it. I was now ready, armed with the truth of God's Word.

I realized that waiting on God for the baptism with the Holy Spirit doesn't have to take ten days, like it did for the disciples. The Holy Spirit has already been given. We can now receive the wonderful infilling by faith, plus action.

"THIS IS THE NIGHT I WILL STEP INTO THE THIRD DIMENSIONAL RELATIONSHIP."

One night, I made the decision. Tonight is the night I receive this blessed experience of being endued with power from on high. So, I first set up my record player with a praise album from Maranatha Music. Some of you younger readers have probably never seen a record player. It's like an antique CD player, only the discs were huge compared to a CD. I knew that it was important to get into an attitude of worship, so I played the music softly in the background.

Then I knelt down between my bedroom and bathroom and began to talk to God, my Father.

"Lord, I have come to you to receive this wonderful experience of being filled with Your Spirit. You said the promise was unto those who are afar off, and here I am, 1975 years afar off. The promise is mine. I love You so much, Father. I can't even find enough English words to thank You for what Jesus has done in my life. I want to serve You all of my life and I need power. I want to praise You in a language I've never learned, so that I can be built up spiritually and empowered to do Your will and purposes. I know I can receive this infilling, this mighty baptism with the Holy Spirit by faith. I know the Holy Spirit doesn't speak in tongues, but prompts the utterance. I know that if I am to receive this gift, I must do it in faith, by believing

165

the Holy Spirit is giving me the utterance and I must begin to speak."

THE HOLY SPIRIT DOESN'T SPEAK IN TONGUES

You see, many people are waiting for the Holy Spirit to speak through them. He's not going to do it. The Bible says, "*They* spoke with tongues." It was "as the Spirit gave the utterance," nonetheless it was *them* that spoke. It was the disciples who spoke in tongues, not the Holy Spirit. They had to believe the Holy Spirit was giving the utterance, but they had to act on their faith and speak it out. So that's what I was determined to do.

I continued my prayer.

"Lord, I love you so very much. My own words are not enough to praise and worship You the way I'd like to. I need the Holy Spirit to help me. Lord, I don't know how this is going to sound, but I'm going to praise You in another language. I just want to thank, praise and magnify You in a way that will satisfy my innermost being."

And I started speaking in another language. It sounded really foolish. The devil instantly came and whispered, "You're making it all up." I responded with a loud voice, "In the Name of Jesus Christ and by His shed Blood, get behind me devil!" And he left.

I continued praying and praising in a strange language. I can see why people call it "gibberish," because frankly that's just what it sounded like to me. But I continued, determined not to stop. I knew I could stop any time I wanted. The Holy Spirit doesn't take away your control. He prompts, He leads, He guides, He gives utterance, but He doesn't push, force, coerce, or shove. He is a perfect Gentleman.

As I was speaking, the words became clearer and more articulate. They were coming from my innermost being, not from my mind. In fact, my intellect was insulted, it all sounded so foolish. But something was happening in my spirit. It was just as Jesus promised, "rivers of living water" coming from my "belly." I just kept moving my lips and making sounds, moving my tongue and trusting that the Holy Spirit was giving the utterance. What a powerful adventure in faith that was.

IT'S REAL AND GENUINE

After about twenty minutes or so, I stopped speaking in tongues. Immediately a wonderful peace enveloped me like I had never before known. Just then, the devil returned and said, "What if all this is really of the devil?" Can you imagine that?

I just knelt there, meditating on the goodness of God. I had a new love for unbelievers and I wanted to reach them for Christ. I had a fresh joy and an unspeakable peace. I thought, "The devil would not give me a love for souls. The devil would not give me joy unspeakable and a peace that passes all understanding. No, this is not from the devil." Warm tears of joy wet my eyes and face.

Every day I prayed with the Spirit *and* with my understanding. My prayer language became easier and much more articulate. I didn't know what language it was, whether it was a language known on earth someplace or only in Heaven, but I didn't really care. I had received an enduement of power from Jesus Himself. I had been baptized with the Holy Spirit.

THE RESULTS AND REWARDS OF BEING BAPTIZED WITH THE HOLY SPIRIT

Within the next couple of months, I led over twenty-five people to Christ. I personally prayed the prayer of salvation with each of them. I started a little Bible study and held baptismal services out at the river for all the converts. Today I am pastor of a wonderful church that has grown to over 4000 worshippers with people coming to Jesus Christ every week. In addition, we have given birth to fifteen other soul-winning churches, reaching their communities with the Good News of Jesus Christ. We are sending and supporting missionaries in over 150 nations of the world.

How did all this happen? It certainly wasn't by the power, holiness, or intelligence of Dave Williams. In fact, it was "not by might, nor by power, but by My Spirit, saith the Lord." [32]

Psalm 127:1 says, "Except the Lord build the house, they labor in vain that build it; except the Lord keep the city, the watchman waketh but in vain."

If it's not the Lord who builds our churches, homes, businesses, and ministries, they won't be built properly. I needed the Lord to build my life, my family, my church, and my ministry. My human intelligence wasn't enough then, and still isn't today. So, I figure, if I want the Lord to build something for me, I better be willing to do things His way. What is His way? To wait for the promise of the Father; the baptism with the Holy Spirit. What marvelous benefits await the Spirit-filled believer. What power exudes from the life of the humble servant who says, "Lord, I can't do it. I need Your power. Fill me to overflowing with your Spirit."

But it doesn't stop there. We must stay filled and occasionally be re-filled.

"*Pentecost. Every time we say, 'I believe in the Holy Spirit,' we mean that we believe that there is a living God able and willing to enter a human personality and change it.*"

— J. B. Phillips

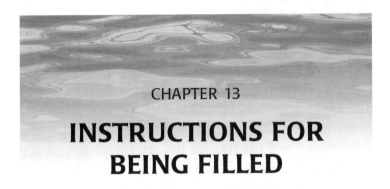

CHAPTER 13

INSTRUCTIONS FOR BEING FILLED

I must confess, I've seen some wild things over the years. I was in one meeting where there was an invitation for believers to receive the baptism with the Holy Spirit.

Probably a hundred people came forward for prayer. I overheard one of the ministers saying to a young lady, "Now, repeat after me. 'Shun-Dah-Mah-Kie-Ah. Shun-Dah-Mah-Kie-Ah.'" He apparently wanted her to repeat his "tongues" so he could report that she had received the baptism with the Holy Spirit. It is no wonder some people are afraid of Pentecostals.

CARNAL COUNTERFEITS

I have heard of others telling people to make up some words to, "prime the pump." So we find people saying, "She-came-on-a-Honda," over and over again, or, "See-ah-my-tie," or, "Taca-Taca-Taca-Taco-Bell." Give me a break. God will not bless this kind of carnality. You want the "real thing," not some carnal counterfeit.

One evening, I led a service with about 1500 people in attendance. I spoke on the baptism with the Holy Spirit and invited believers to come forward to the altar and be filled. About 150 people came forward for prayer that night. After giving some instructions, I prayed, and all but two received this glorious baptism, complete with the initial evidence of speaking in other tongues. And it only took a few minutes.

WHAT HOLDS PEOPLE BACK?

Why is it that some believers ask, but never receive? Why is that so? I believe the answer is twofold. First, they may need to break through many years of false teaching and tradition that has cluttered their minds. Second, they may not be putting action to their faith by speaking forth in tongues. They may be waiting for a special feeling. But the feeling may or may not come until *first* there is an *act* of faith.

MY SIMPLE INSTRUCTIONS

Let me give you an overview of the instructions I give people when leading them into receiving this miraculous gift.

■ *Number 1 — First I lay the Scriptural groundwork.*

    A. The Great Commission (Matthew 28:18-20). Jesus told His disciples to teach their converts "to observe *all things* whatsoever I commanded you." In Luke 24, during his final message, Jesus commanded the disciples to "tarry ye in the city of Jerusalem *until* ye be endued with power from on high." Acts 1:4, 5, and 8 verifies the fact that Jesus was talking about the baptism with the Holy Spirit. Mark 16:17 tells that one of the signs for believers would be that, "they shall speak with new tongues." Taken with the other related Scriptures, we know He is referring to the enduement of power; the baptism with the Holy Spirit.

    B. I quickly take them through the book of Acts to show them what happened when the first century believers received the infilling with the Holy Spirit. They spoke with tongues (Acts 2:4; Acts 10:44-46; Acts 19:6). To prepare for opposition from those who say that the speaking in tongues is not mentioned in two other accounts, I explain that in Paul's account of being filled with the Holy Spirit, it doesn't mention that he spoke in tongues. Yet, by reading 1 Corinthians 14:18, we know he did because he said, "I thank my God I speak with tongues more than ye all." The other case was in Acts 8 when the revival broke out in Samaria. It doesn't say they spoke with tongues, but it doesn't say they didn't either. Simon, the sorcerer, saw something when believers were filled with the Holy Spirit and he wanted to buy that power. What did he see? Well, if we are going to be true to the Scriptural and historic pattern, it had to be that he saw something supernatural happening. It obviously was the initial gift of tongues that Simon saw.

C. I try to point out that praying "in the spirit" or "with the spirit" is defined by St. Paul, as praying mysteries, without our understanding; or in other words, tongues. When you read the terms "praying in (or with) the Holy Ghost," in other parts of the New Testament, it is referring to praying in tongues (languages you have never learned). See 1 Corinthians 14:2, 15 which defines "speaking in the Spirit," (Ephesians 5:18-19; Jude 20).

■ *Number 2 — After I have walked the candidates through the New Testament, I try to clear up some of their fears.*

A. I assure them that they won't get a demon by seeking God for this (Luke 11:9-13).

    B. I assure them that they won't curse Jesus while speaking in tongues (1 Corinthians 12:3).

■ *Number 3 — Next, I give them the prerequisites for receiving.*

    A. You must turn from the life-style of sin and place your trust in Jesus Christ. You must be born again (John 3:3-7).

    B. You must desire to be filled with the Holy Spirit, because you desire to obey God, serve God, and worship God in a satisfying way (John 4:21-24; Matthew 28:20; Mark 11:24; Luke 24:49).

■ *Number 4 — Then, I will sometimes explain and refute the false concepts concerning the baptism with the Holy Spirit.*

    A. "It happens at the point of salvation." I show them that it never — not once — happened that way in the Bible.

    B. "The Holy Ghost will take you over and it will be uncontrollable." This is nonsense. God will not violate your will. That's why Paul said, "I *will* pray with the spirit, and I *will* pray with my understanding." It is an act of the human will; not something uncontrollable that will put you in a trance or dominate all your motor functions.

C. *"Sometimes you need to tarry a long time."* This is typically an excuse used by the person who never puts action to his faith. Yes, the disciples had to "tarry" until the day of Pentecost, but after that we have no Biblical record that believers had to just tarry, waiting around for the event to happen. It's true, before you begin to launch your ministry, you should wait until you receive the baptism with the Holy Spirit, but you can receive the experience right this minute if you will put action to your faith.

Some folks say, "I don't believe in this newfangled way of receiving the baptism with the Holy Ghost. I believe we need to get back to the old 'tarrying times.'" Well, I believe in waiting on the Lord. Isaiah 40:31 offers tremendous benefits to the believer who will wait upon the Lord. But when something is clearly promised by God; something we can have *now* by faith, I'm not going to wait. Yes, I love waiting on God, in His presence, during times of prayer, worship and intercession, but I'm not content to wait for something that is already mine.

D. *"You'll see the words in your mind that God wants you to speak."* No, this is not correct. The baptism with the Holy Spirit is a spiritual experience, not a mental experience. One of the great purposes of speaking in tongues is to put your mind where it belongs — in second place to your spirit.

E. *"The Holy Ghost will speak through you."* This is another one of those erroneous ideas that keeps a lot of people from receiving. They are waiting for a voice to speak through them, but it won't happen.

The Holy Spirit doesn't speak in tongues. He gives the utterance, but you are the one that speaks. "The Holy Ghost came on them; and *they* spake with tongues and prophesied," (Acts 19:5). Who spoke in tongues? *They* did. It was not the Holy Ghost. Paul wrote, "I thank my God, I *speak* with tongues..." (1 Corinthians 14:18). Who spoke in tongues? Paul did. Again, it was not the Holy Ghost.

■ *Number 5 — Next, I warn the candidates for the baptism with the Holy Spirit of the devil's strategies to discourage them.*

A. *When you begin to speak in tongues, the devil will likely say, "That's just you speaking!"* Well, he's partially right. It is *you* speaking, but it's the Holy Spirit giving you the utterance. So, in essence, it's not "just you" speaking. That's why Paul talked about praying *with* the Spirit. Again, you do the natural, and the Holy Spirit will do the "super," and together it's a supernatural transaction.

B. *The devil will probably tell you that you are, "making it all up," when you begin to speak in supernatural tongues.* It's his ploy to get you to stop. Don't stop. Keep praying in those strange sounding tongues and you will find a fresh anointing of power come over your life.

C. *The devil will probably bring to your mind some of the erroneous teachings you've heard over the years, hoping to destroy your faith.* He may suggest, "You are really messing up. This was for the apostles only. You have no promise from God for this. Stop now before judgement falls on you." What? No promise? We have more than a promise, we also have a command to be filled. Jesus told his disciples to receive this miraculous baptism with the Holy Spirit, and Peter assured us that the promise was for us, our children, and those who are afar off (Acts 2:38).

■ *Number 6 — I tell the believers wanting to be filled that God has already given the gift of the Holy Spirit.*

He has made this wonderful baptism available to us now. You don't have to beg. Just shout for joy and begin praising God in a language you've never learned.

■ *Number 7 — At this juncture I usually tell people that sometimes it is helpful to groan in the Spirit first (Romans 8:26).*

After groaning, then begin moving your lips and tongue, trusting the Holy Spirit to give you the prompting. I tell them not to wait for a special feeling. That may come or it may not come, it doesn't matter either way, because this is a faith event, not merely an emotional occasion.

■ *Number 8 — I tell everyone who has asked to receive the baptism with the Holy Spirit to begin worshipping and focusing on Jesus.*

Sometimes I'll have soft worship music playing in the background, but it is not necessary. I instruct them to focus on Jesus, for He is the Baptizer with the Holy Spirit.

■ *Number 9 — Finally, I tell them that the moment I lay my hands on them, the Holy Spirit will give them the utterance to speak in tongues.*

I instruct them to cease all native language praises (in other words for most Americans, this would mean to speak no more words in English for the time being), and immediately begin to praise God in tongues. I am honest, and tell them it will sound foolish, but to do it anyway. I once again go over the benefits of this experience with them, reminding them that our spirit needs to ascend above our minds. Since the word "spirit" in the Greek language is the same as "air" or "breath," I sometimes will instruct the candidates to take a deep breath when they feel my hands touch them, then begin to praise in other languages.

■ *Number 10 — Now it is time to receive.*

As the worshippers are praising the Lord, focusing on Jesus Christ, I will slowly walk through the crowd and, one by one, lay my hands on them and say, "Receive the infilling of the Holy Spirit." Nothing happened to me when I was twelve years old in that Lutheran confirmation ceremony when the pastor said those words, but today is a different day. Nearly 100% of those who come to us for this baptism in power, receive what they came for within just a few minutes.

You don't need someone to lay hands on you to receive this blessing. The laying on of hands, however, may assist you by giving you a specific point to release your faith.

Perhaps you are a believer who just wants the ability to worship God in a deeper dimension. Jesus said these words to a little woman two thousand years ago:

> Jesus saith unto her, Woman, believe me, the hour cometh, when ye shall neither in this mountain, nor yet at Jerusalem, worship the Father. Ye worship ye know not what: we know what we worship: for salvation is of the Jews. But the hour cometh, and now is, when the true worshippers shall worship the Father in spirit and in truth: for the Father seeketh such to worship him. God *is* a Spirit: and they that worship him must worship *him* in spirit and in truth.
>
> — John 4:21-24

Why wait? You can receive in your home or in your back yard. You can receive this wonderful gift at a Bible study group, or even in your garage or pole barn.

DO YOU WANT THE ANOINTING OF POWER?

Do you really want an anointing of power for your life and ministry? Do you want a deep, fruitful relationship with the Holy Spirit? Do you want gifts of the Holy Spirit to flow through your life? Do you really want to come into the third dimensional relationship with the Holy Spirit? If so, ask God to fill you now with His Spirit. Start praising Him in another language you have never learned, trusting that the Holy Spirit is giving you the utterance.

You may think the gift of tongues is strange sounding at first. But don't judge it until you see the fruit of your being baptized with the Holy Spirit. A new love will be shed abroad in your heart (Romans 5:5), a new anointing will shine in your life. And, best of all, you'll become more and more fulfilled in your worship of God.

Are you ready for the adventure? Are you ready for the third dimensional relationship with the Holy Spirit? Then receive the gift *now.*

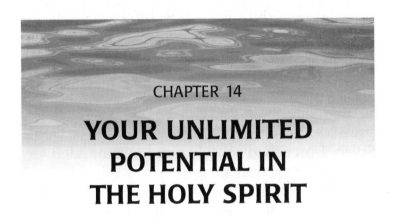

CHAPTER 14

YOUR UNLIMITED POTENTIAL IN THE HOLY SPIRIT

Years ago, a young Methodist woman whom I'll call Mary, would visit our church from another city. She was in love with one of the young Spirit-filled men in our congregation, so naturally she enjoyed visiting. But she had an embarassing medical problem — a skin disorder.

When we'd talk to her about God's healing gifts, or about the baptism with the Holy Spirit, she would reject our sincere concern for her. She had never been taught about speaking in tongues and had no doubt heard some negative things about the practice, thus she shied away from the supernatural. But the supernatural is precisely what she needed.

After a few months, the enthusiasm of our members began to rub off on Mary. Someone said if you hang around with Pentecostals very long, you'll end up becoming one! One preacher put it this way: "If you keep walking on a slippery bank by the river, it won't be long before you slip right down into the river." Such was the case with Mary.

It was a Sunday evening. The Lord had impressed upon me to speak on matters of God's Spirit. I preached on salvation, healing, deliverance, and the baptism in the Holy Spirit. When I gave the invitation for people to come to Christ, I'd say about 40 people responded and came forward to pray the "sinner's prayer" with me. Then when I offered to pray with others to receive healing, deliverance, or the baptism in the Holy Spirit, people flooded down to the altar. The entire front of the auditorium was packed shoulder to shoulder with people.

To my surprise, Mary was standing there. It seemed that being in our church for the past few months had softened her heart and made her realize her need for the Holy Spirit's power. I asked our associate ministers and elders to help me pray with all the people. When one of the ministers prayed with Mary, she fell backwards onto the floor as if struck by electricity. As she lay there on the floor, heavenly languages started pouring out of her mouth. She was weeping, rejoicing, and praying in tongues. Jesus had baptized her with the Holy Ghost.

That week she drove back to the little village she had lived in all her life until she went to college. She attended the little denominational church she has been raised in all through her childhood and teenage years. She was telling some of the older women what had happened to her, and what she had seen happening in our church. The older ladies pulled her aside and told her in a kind whisper,

> "Oh, we remember the days when our church was just like that. People were being saved every week. We'd pray for sick people all the time and witness many divine healings in those days. Why, most of the people in our church spoke in tongues back then. But over the past fifty years or so, fewer and fewer were meeting Jesus here. We started hearing the preachers say doctors were the only ones with the gift of healing, and fewer and fewer people were healed and the gifts of the Holy Spirit seemed to quit operating. Now look. I haven't seen anybody saved in this church in over twenty years. Nobody ever gets healed anymore and you never see anybody struck by the Holy Spirit's joy."

LOSING THE POWER

That is sad. What is it that causes a vibrant church to lose its power, its anointing, its joy? I believe the reason is common neglect. Neglecting the gift that God has given us. Churches grow cold, stale, and powerless by ignoring the Holy Spirit and His present-day ministry. Paul exhorted Timothy, a young pastor, to not let this happen.

> **Wherefore I put thee in remembrance that thou stir up the gift of God, which is in thee by the putting on of my hands.**
>
> **— 2 Timothy 1:6**

CONQUER YOUR FEARS WITH FAITH

Apparently Timothy, through fear and intimidation, was allowing his gift to be buried instead of exercising it for the good of the church.

> **For God hath not given us the spirit of fear; but of power, and of love, and of a sound mind.**
>
> **— 2 Timothy 1:7**

Many people allow fear to derail their faith. Fear and faith cannot dwell together. They are both the same kind of force, so to speak, but going in different directions. In other words, fear is faith in reverse. Faith believes and acts upon the promises of God. Fear believes and acts upon something other than the Word of God.

Mary conquered her fears by acting upon God's promise to fill her with the blessed Holy Ghost. And as a witness to the authenticity of her experience, she had a new boldness in witnessing for Christ. But that is not the end of the story.

Within just a few weeks, Mary's skin disorder vanished. Not only did she receive the miracle gift of the Holy Ghost that night, but God began to work in her a gift of healing as well. I don't know why, but it seems that God chose tongues to be the gateway gift to all the rest. Imagine that. This gift that is the, "least of all gifts," God chose to be the starting point into a life of supernatural adventure.

THIS IS ONLY THE BEGINNING

The baptism with the Holy Spirit is only the beginning. If you have received this wonderful gift and yet see no further manifestations of the supernatural in your life, if you seem to have grown cold with no overflowing joy, peace, love, and power, perhaps it is because you have ignored or neglected your gift. Perhaps you once prayed in tongues, but never continued.

If you miss out on the secret of praying and worshipping in the Spirit, you are missing something that is immeasurable in value. If you are only praying with your understanding, your mind is active, but your spirit is starving. Begin, once again, to stir up the gift of God and pray both with your understanding and with the Spirit (in tongues).

The third dimensional relationship with the Holy Spirit is a rousing adventure. It's more breathtaking than being an explorer or a globetrotter. Living in the third dimension with the Holy Spirit is more soul stirring than being a mountain climber, or wild game hunter. The third dimensional relationship with the Holy Spirit is the mode for walking with God. The first century believers understood this.

THE POWER OF THE FIRST CENTURY CHURCH

Is it any wonder the first church saw such phenomenal signs and wonders and diverse miracles of the Holy Ghost? It wasn't because of who the apostles were. They were just ordinary people like you and me. Supernatural signs followed them everywhere, not because of who they were, but because of Who was leading and directing their lives and ministries.

Is it a mystery as to why the first church experienced such explosive growth? 3000 came to Christ in one day.[33] A few days later, another 5000.[34] Sick and diseased people wanted to be thrown into Peter's shadow, with the faith they'd be healed.[35] People were healed and demons were ejected by the tangible power in Paul's handkerchiefs.[36] Laymen, like Stephen and Phillip, possessed amazing anointings of the Holy Spirit to achieve greater things than they could ever do in their own powers. [37]

The first century church was filled, led, and directed by the Holy Spirit. And when the twenty-first century church becomes filled, led, and directed by the same Holy Spirit, we'll once again enjoy explosive church growth, revival, healing, miracles, signs and wonders.

> Then they that gladly received his word were baptized: and the same day there were added *unto them* about three thousand souls.
>
> — Acts 2:41

> And believers were the more added to the Lord, multitudes both of men and women. Insomuch that they brought forth the sick into the streets, and laid *them* on beds and couches, that at the least the shadow of Peter passing by might overshadow some of them. There came also a multitude *out* of the cities round about unto Jerusalem, bringing sick folks, and them which were vexed with unclean spirits: and they were healed every one.
>
> — Acts 5:14-16

> And the word of God increased; and the number of the disciples multiplied in Jerusalem greatly; and a great company of the priests were obedient to the faith.
>
> — Acts 6:7

> Then Philip went down to the city of Samaria, and preached Christ unto them. And the people with one accord gave heed unto those things which Philip spake, hearing and seeing the miracles which he did.

For unclean spirits, crying with loud voice, came out of many that were possessed *with them*: and many taken with palsies, and that were lame, were healed. And there was great joy in that city.

— Acts 8:5-8

And the next sabbath day came almost the whole city together to hear the word of God.

— Acts 13:44

And there sat a certain man at Lystra, impotent in his feet, being a cripple from his mother's womb, who never had walked: The same heard Paul speak: who stedfastly beholding him, and perceiving that he had faith to be healed, Said with a loud voice, Stand upright on thy feet. And he leaped and walked.

— Acts 14:8-10

And so were the churches established in the faith, and increased in number daily.

— Acts 16:5

And God wrought special miracles by the hands of Paul: So that from his body were brought unto the sick handkerchiefs or aprons, and the diseases departed from them, and the evil spirits went out of them.

— Acts 19:11-12

These are just a few of the historic results of walking with the Holy Spirit in the third dimensional relationship. Some cessationist theologians will try to tell you that you can't take doctrine from the Book of Acts because it is a record of history.

But Paul told Timothy that *all Scripture* is profitable for doctrine.

> All scripture *is* given by inspiration of God, and *is* profitable for doctrine, for reproof, for correction, for instruction in righteousness: That the man of God may be perfect, thoroughly furnished unto all good works.
>
> — 2 Timothy 3:16-17

A TEENAGER'S TESTIMONY

One of the young ladies in our church, Linda, just 18 years old, went to spend a year with a teen ministry in Texas. She and her friend Anna came upon a seventy-year old lady in a wheel chair who hadn't walked a step in eight years since having a stroke. They asked the lady if they could pray for her. The girls had prayed both in the spirit (tongues) and with their understanding that day and were endued with power from Heaven.

The lady asked for prayer. They laid their hands on the crippled woman, and commanded, "Rise up and walk!" The lady hopped up from her wheelchair and walked! The lady's daughter, who witnessed this miracle, broke down into tears and asked the girls if she could receive Jesus Christ too. The power of God demonstrated through Spirit-filled believers will always cause others to come to Christ.

Later the same day, Linda found a young man, apparently Oriental, whose legs were paralyzed from a motorcycle accident. Linda began praying in tongues. The startled man looked up and asked, "You know Cantonese?" Linda shook her head and answered, "No, I'm sorry, I don't." The man looked confused because he heard her praying in perfect Cantonese as she was praying in her prayer language. A few moments later feeling came to the man's legs and he was able to sense touch for the first time in three years. He had received a healing.

That evening, the teen group was gathered for a prayer meeting. A visiting Christian woman from China was in the group as a guest. She knew very little English; just enough to communicate, but not very clearly. She wanted to say a few words to encourage the teens, but knew that with her limited English, it wouldn't come out the way she wanted, so she indicated that she needed an interpreter.

The young people began to pray and worship the Lord. Linda was praising God fervently in tongues, as were many of the others.[38] The Chinese lady indicated to one of the prayer leaders that Linda could be her interpreter. When they approached Linda about it, she was surprised. "I don't speak Cantonese at all," she said. Yet the lady from China insisted that Linda, in fact, was speaking in beautiful, perfect Cantonese as she was praying in the Spirit.

Is your life lacking adventure? Are your results like the ones the first century church saw?

Maybe you could use a fresh infilling with the Holy Spirit. As I understand the Bible, the infilling with the Holy Spirit is not to be a one-time event. In Acts chapter four, we find the Spirit-filled disciples praying. After they prayed, they were all filled with the Holy Ghost again and were able to speak God's Word with a fresh boldness.

> And when they had prayed, the place was shaken where they were assembled together; and they were all filled with the Holy Ghost, and they spake the word of God with boldness.
>
> — Acts 4:31

A Scripture I've mentioned before, relating to the need to be re-filled from time to time is Ephesians 5:18, 19.

> And be not drunk with wine, wherein is excess; but be filled with the Spirit; Speaking to yourselves in psalms and hymns and spiritual songs, singing and making melody in your heart to the Lord;
>
> — Ephesians 5:18-19

The Greek structure of this verse reads like this: "Be [constantly] being filled with the Spirit."

KEEP BEING FILLED WITH THE HOLY SPIRIT

This tells us that being filled with the Holy Spirit is not supposed to be just a one time memorable episode. Being filled with the Holy Spirit is meant to become a way of life. The word "filled" in the Greek language is defined as: "to be crammed full; no room for anything else." When you are filled with the Holy Spirit, there will be no room for self, works of the flesh, or human pride. God will get all the glory from a truly Spirit-filled life.

If it has been a while since you have prayed in tongues, make a commitment now to pray often in the Spirit. You can do it in your car, on your way to and from work, or school. You can go to sleep at night praying in the Spirit, and wake up in the morning praying in the Spirit. Remember, pray in the Spirit, and with your understanding. Stir up the gift of God. Start gaining ground by living in the Holy Spirit's third dimension. When you don't know how to pray in a situation, pray in tongues.

UNLIMITED POTENTIAL IN THE THIRD DIMENSION

What would happen if every believer in our nation were filled with the Spirit, walked in the Spirit, and prayed in the Spirit, as the Scriptures teach? It would only be a matter of a few years, maybe only a few months, before the greatest revival in all of history would sweep across our land. Our nation, schools, businesses, churches and neighborhoods would all come under a divine cloud of glory, and we'd be ready to meet Jesus face to face.

Why don't you decide now to live as a third-dimensional Christian. One who not only has the Holy Spirit with you, and in you, but *upon* you as well. Together, we'll see miracles and win the lost speedily. Be filled now.

Endnotes

1 1 Corinthians 12:13

2 John 14:17

3 Enduement is a Greek word in English letters. It means to be clothed with, for example, a robe. "Clothed with anointing," "clothed with power," etc.

4 Luke 24:49; Acts 1:4, 5, 8

5 The Holy Spirit convicts but does not condemn. The sinner is already condemned. The Holy Spirit, representing Jesus Christ, works to gently "pull" the sinner to Christ. John 3:16, 17; 16:8-11

6 Romans 3:23; 6:23

7 1 Corinthians 12:13

8 Matthew 3:11; Acts 1:4-8

9 Global Prayer Center, 202 S. Creyts Road, Lansing, MI 48917, 517-327-PRAY

10 John 7:38,39

11 W.E. Vines Complete Expository Dictionary of Old and New Testament Words

12 Through the Bible Radio Program with Dr. J. Vernon McGee

13 1 Corinthians 13:9, 10

14 The Holy Spirit and You, Father Dennis & Rita Bennett, Logos Publishing

15 Jackie, Rhonda Gillies' father, Easter 2000

16 Acts 17:6

17 Acts 5:28

18 Maranatha! Music, Come To The Waters, Children of the Day 1971

[19] History of the Pentecostal Movement, Vinson Synan PhD. 1996, Oral Roberts University

[20] Morning Star Prophetic Bulletin, May 2000

[21] Deception, Delusion and Destruction, Dave Williams, Mount Hope Books, 1991

[22] How Great Soul Winners Were Filled with The Holy Spirit c. 1949 Dr. John R. Rice Sword of the Lord Publications, Murfreesboro, TN

[23] The Conspiracy Against the Supernatural, Dr. Jack Deere, Global Harvest Ministries Video, 1997

[24] Before We Kill and Eat You, H.B. Garlock, CFN Books, Dallas, 1974

[25] 1 Corinthians 14:13, 27-28

[26] The Conspiracy Against the Supernatural, Dr. Jack Deere, Global Harvest Ministries Video, 1997

[27] Getting to Know Your Heavenly Father, Dave Williams, Mount Hope Books, 1989

[28] John 3:3-7

[29] Acts 2:39

[30] Word for Today, Costa Mesa, California, Holy Spirit Series by Chuck Smith

[31] The Holy Spirit and You, Father Dennis & Rita Bennett, Logos Publishing

[32] Zechariah 4:6

[33] Acts 2:41

[34] Acts 4:4

[35] Acts 5:15

[36] Acts 19:11, 12

[37] Acts 6:8 and Acts 8:5-8

[38] 1 Corinthians 14:15

About The Author

Dave Williams is pastor of Mount Hope Church and International Outreach Ministries, with world headquarters in Lansing, Michigan. He has served for over 20 years, leading the church in Lansing from 226 to over 4000 today. Dave sends trained ministers into unreached cities to establish disciple-making churches, and, as a result, today has "branch" churches in the United States, Philippines, and in Africa.

Dave is the founder and president of Mount Hope Bible Training Institute, a fully accredited institute for training ministers and lay people for the work of the ministry. He has authored 45 books including the fifteen-time best seller, *The Start of Something Wonderful* (with over 2,000,000 books sold), and more recently, *The Miracle Results of Fasting*, and *The Road To Radical Riches*.

The Pacesetter's Path telecast is Dave's weekly television program seen over a syndicated network of secular stations, and nationally over the Sky Angel satellite system. Dave has produced over 125 audio cassette programs including the nationally acclaimed School of Pacesetting Leadership which is being used as a training program in churches around the United States, and in Bible Schools in South Africa and the Philippines. He is a popular speaker at conferences, seminars, and conventions. His speaking ministry has taken him across America, Africa, Europe, Asia, and other parts of the world.

Along with his wife, Mary Jo, Dave established The Dave and Mary Jo Williams Charitable Mission (Strategic Global Mission), a mission's ministry for providing scholarships to pioneer pastors and grants to inner-city children's ministries.

Dave's articles and reviews have appeared in national magazines such as *Advance, The Pentecostal Evangel, Ministries Today, The Lansing Magazine, The Detroit Free Press* and others. Dave, as a private pilot, flies for fun. He is married, has two grown children, and lives in Delta Township, Michigan.

You may write to Pastor Dave Williams:

P.O. Box 80825

Lansing, MI 48908-0825

Please include your special prayer requests when you write, or you may call the Mount Hope Global Prayer Center anytime: (517) 327-PRAY

DECAPOLIS
PUBLISHING

For a catalog of products, call:

1-517-321-2780 or

1-800-888-7284

or visit us on the web at:

www.mounthopechurch.org

For Your Spiritual Growth

Here's the help you need for your spiritual journey. These books will encourage you, and give you guidance as you seek to draw close to Jesus and learn of Him. Prepare yourself for fantastic growth!

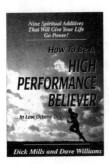

HOW TO BE A HIGH PERFORMANCE BELIEVER
Pour in the nine spiritual additives for real power in your Christian life.

SECRET OF POWER WITH GOD
Tap into the real power with God; the power of prayer. It will change your life!

THE NEW LIFE...
You can get off to a great start on your exciting life with Jesus! Prepare for something wonderful.

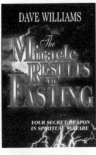

MIRACLE RESULTS OF FASTING
You can receive MIRACLE benefits, spiritually and physically, with this practical Christian discipline.

WHAT TO DO IF YOU MISS THE RAPTURE
If you miss the Rapture, there may still be hope, but you need to follow these clear survival tactics.

THE AIDS PLAGUE
Is there hope? Yes, but only Jesus can bring a total and lasting cure to AIDS.

These and other books available from Dave Williams and:

DECAPOLIS PUBLISHING

For Your Spiritual Growth

Here's the help you need for your spiritual journey. These books will encourage you, and give you guidance as you seek to draw close to Jesus and learn of Him. Prepare yourself for fantastic growth!

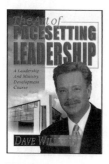

THE ART OF PACESETTING LEADERSHIP
You can become a successful leader with this proven leadership development course.

GIFTS THAT SHAPE YOUR LIFE
Learn which ministry best fits you, and discover your God-given personality gifts, as well as the gifts of others.

GROWING UP IN OUR FATHER'S FAMILY
You can have a family relationship with your heavenly father. Learn how God cares for you.

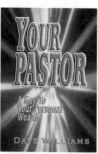

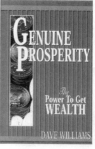

SUPERNATURAL SOULWINNING
How will we reach our family, friends, and neighbors in this short time before Christ's return?

YOUR PASTOR: A KEY TO YOUR PERSONAL WEALTH
By honoring your pastor you can actually be setting yourself up for a financial blessing from God!

GENUINE PROSPERITY
Learn what it means to be truly prosperous! God gives us the power to get wealth!

These and other books available from Dave Williams and:

DECAPOLIS PUBLISHING

For Your Spiritual Growth

Here's the help you need for your spiritual journey. These books will encourage you, and give you guidance as you seek to draw close to Jesus and learn of Him. Prepare yourself for fantastic growth!

SOMEBODY OUT THERE NEEDS YOU
Along with the gift of salvation comes the great privilege of spreading the gospel of Jesus Christ.

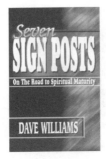

SEVEN SIGNPOSTS TO SPIRITUAL MATURITY
Examine your life to see where you are on the road to spiritual maturity.

THE PASTORS PAY
How much is your pastor worth? Who should set his pay? Discover the scriptural guidelines for paying your pastor.

DECEPTION, DELUSION & DESTRUCTION
Recognize spiritual deception and unmask spiritual blindness.

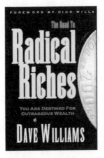

THE ROAD TO RADICAL RICHES
Are you ready to jump from "barely getting by" to Gods plan for putting you on the road to Radical Riches?

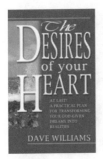

THE DESIRES OF YOUR HEART
Yes, Jesus wants to give you the desires of your heart, and make them realities.

These and other books available from Dave Williams and:

DECAPOLIS PUBLISHING

Expanding Your Faith

These exciting audio teaching series will help you to grow and mature in your walk with Christ. Get ready for amazing new adventures in faith!

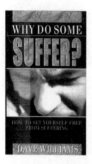

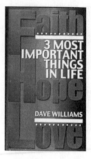

WHY DO SOME SUFFER

Find out why some people seem to have suffering in their lives, and find out how to avoid it in your life.

SIN'S GRIP

Learn how you can avoid the vice-like grip of sin and it's fatal enticements that hold people captive.

FAITH, HOPE, & LOVE

Listen and let these three "most important things in life" change you.

PSALM 91
THE PROMISE OF PROTECTION
Everyone is looking for protection in these perilous times. God promises protection for those who rest in Him.

DEVELOPING
THE SPIRIT OF A CONQUEROR
You can be a conqueror through Christ! Also, find out how to *keep* those things that you have conquered.

YOUR SPECTACULAR MIND
Identify wrong thinking and negative influences in your life.

These and other audio tapes available from Dave Williams and:

DECAPOLIS PUBLISHING

Expanding Your Faith

These exciting audio teaching series will help you to grow and mature in your walk with Christ. Get ready for amazing new adventures in faith!

ABC's OF SUCCESS AND HAPPINESS

FORGIVENESS
The miracle remedy for many of life's problems is found in this basic key for living.

UNTANGLING YOUR TROUBLES
You can be a "trouble untangler" with the help of Jesus!

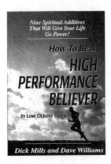

HOW TO BE A HIGH PERFORMANCE BELIEVER
Put in the nine spiritual additives to help run your race and get the prize!

BEING A DISCIPLE AND MAKING DISCIPLES
You can learn to be a "disciple maker" to almost anyone.

HOW TO HELP YOUR PASTOR & CHURCH SUCCEED
You can be an integral part of your church's & pastor's success.

These and other audio tapes available from Dave Williams and:

DECAPOLIS PUBLISHING

More Products by Dave Williams

BOOK Title	Price
The New Life — The Start Of Something Wonderful	$1.95
End Times Bible Prophecy	$4.95
Seven Sign Posts On the Road To Spiritual Maturity	$4.95
Somebody Out There Needs You	$4.95
Growing Up In Our Father's Family	$4.95
Grief & Mourning	$7.95
The World Beyond — Mysteries Of Heaven	$7.95
The Secret Of Power With God	$7.95
What To Do If You Miss the Rapture	$9.95
Genuine Prosperity	$9.95
The Miracle Results Of Fasting	$9.95
How To Be A High Performance Believer	$9.95
Gifts That Shape Your Life & Change Your World	$10.95
Road To Radical Riches	$19.95

CD Title	Num. of CDs	Price
Middle East Crisis	1	$12.00
Setting Our Houses In Order	1	$12.00
Too Much Baggage?	1	$12.00
Jesus Loves Sinners	1	$12.00
How To Get Your Breakthrough	1	$12.00
Amazing Power Of Desire	1	$12.00
Wounded Spirit	1	$12.00
The Attack On America (Sept. 11, 2001)	1	$12.00
Radical Wealth	5	$60.00

VIDEO Title	Num. of Videos	Price
What To Do When You Are Going Through Hell	1	$19.95
Acres Of Diamonds — The Valley Of Baca	1	$19.95
120 Elite Warriors	1	$19.95
What To Do If You Miss the Rapture	1	$19.95
Regaining Your Spiritual Momentum	1	$19.95
Herbs For Health	1	$19.95
TheDestructive Power Of Legalism	1	$19.95
4 Ugly Worms Of Judgment	1	$19.95
Grief and Mourning	1	$19.95
Breaking the Power Of Poverty	1	$19.95
Triple Benefits Of Fasting	1	$19.95
Why Some Are Not Healed	2	$39.95
Miracle Results Of Fasting	3	$59.95
ABCs Of Success and Happiness	3	$59.95
Gifts That Shape Your Life and Change Your World	5	$99.95

AUDIO Title	Num. of Tapes	Price
Lonely In the Midst Of a Crowd	1	$6.00
How To Get Anything You Want	1	$6.00
Untangling Your Troubles	2	$12.00
Healing Principles In the Ministry Of Jesus	2	$12.00
Acres Of Diamonds — The Valley Of Baca	2	$12.00
Finding Peace	2	$12.00
Criticize & Judge	2	$12.00
Judgment On America	2	$12.00
Triple Benefits Of Fasting	2	$12.00
Global Confusion	2	$12.00
The Cure For a Broken Heart	2	$12.00
Help! I'm Getting Older	2	$12.00
Regaining Your Spiritual Momentum	2	$12.00
The Destructive Power Of Legalism	2	$12.00
Three Most Important Things In Life	3	$18.00
The Final Series	3	$18.00
The Mysteries of Heaven	3	$18.00
Dave Williams' Crash Course In Intercessory Prayer	3	$18.00
Forgiveness — The Miracle Remedy	4	$24.00
How Long Until the End	4	$24.00
What To Do When You Feel Weak and Defeated	4	$24.00
Sin's Grip	4	$24.00
Why Some Are Not Healed	4	$24.00
Bible Cures	4	$24.00
Belial	4	$24.00
God is Closer Than You Think	5	$30.00
Decoding the Apocalypse	5	$30.00
Winning Your Inner Conflict	5	$30.00
Radical Wealth	5	$30.00
Violent Action For Your Wealth	5	$30.00
The Presence Of God	6	$36.00
Your Spectacular Mind	6	$36.00
The Miracle Results of Fasting	6	$36.00
Developing the Spirit Of a Conqueror	6	$36.00
Why Do Some Suffer	6	$36.00
Overcoming Life's Adversities	6	$36.00
Faith Steps	6	$36.00
ABCs For Success & Happiness	6	$36.00
The Best Of Dave Williams	6	$36.00
How To Help Your Pastor & Church Succeed	8	$48.00
Being a Disciple & Making Disciples	8	$48.00
High Performance Believer	8	$48.00
True Or False	8	$48.00
The End Times	8	$48.00
The Beatitudes — Success 101	8	$48.00
Hearing the Voice Of God	10	$60.00
Gifts That Shape Your Life — Personality Gifts	10	$60.00
Gifts That Shape Your Life & Change Your World — Ministry Gifts	10	$60.00
Daniel Parts 1 & 2 (Both parts 6 tapes each)	12	$72.00
Roadblocks To Your Radical Wealth	12	$72.00
Revelation Parts 1 & 2 (part 1 - 6 tapes; part 2 - 8 tapes)	14	$84.00

Mount Hope Ministries

Mount Hope Missions & International Outreach
Care Ministries, Deaf Ministries
& Support Groups
Access to Christ for the Physically Impaired
Community Outreach Ministries
Mount Hope Youth Ministries
Mount Hope Bible Training Institute
The Hope Store and Decapolis Publishing
The Pacesetter's Path Telecast
The Pastor's Minute Radio Broadcast
Mount Hope Children's Ministry
Champions Club and Sidewalk Sunday School
The Saturday Care Clinic

When you're facing a struggle and need someone to pray with you, please call us at (517) 321-CARE or (517) 327-PRAY. We have pastors on duty 24 hours a day. We know you hurt sometimes and need a pastor, a minister, or a prayer partner. There will be ministers and prayer partners here for you.

If you'd like to write, we'd be honored to pray for you. Our address is:

MOUNT HOPE CHURCH
202 S. CREYTS RD.
LANSING, MI 48917
(517) 321-CARE or (517) 321-2780
FAX (517)321-6332
TDD (517) 321-8200

www.mounthopechurch.org

email: mhc@mounthopechurch.org

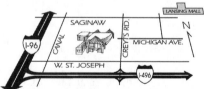

West of the Lansing Mall, on Creyts at Michigan Ave.